MW00397912

Uncompromising *Purity*

(IT'S NOT JUST A
"GUY" PROBLEM)

Kelsey Skoch with Everett Fritz
Foreword by Sarah Swafford

Totus Tuus
— P R E S S —
2019

Uncompromising Purity
© 2019 Totus Tuus Press, LLC.

Published by Totus Tuus Press, LLC.
P.O. Box 5065
Scottsdale, AZ 85261
www.totustuuspress.com

Cover by Devin Schadt
Interior by Russell Graphic Design

Printed in the United States of America

Paperback ISBN: 978-1-944578-01-5
E book ISBN: 978-1-944578-02-2

FOREWORD

For years I have been thinking about how much I wished someone would write this book, even asking people directly if they felt called to write it. I knew it had to be written by the right people, people who would be able to speak to this sensitive and challenging topic in a clear, honest, and effective way. I truly thank God that Kelsey and Everett have stepped forward to write this book.

Women's battle with pornography and masturbation is real; it is definitely not just a man's issue. Early in my ministry, a few women each year would email me or pull me aside and confide that they were struggling with this issue; now almost every week by email—and almost every time I speak—women of all ages thank me profusely for bringing this issue up because they, too, are steeped in this fight.

The difficulty is often a silent one. Many women go years without breathing a word about it to another soul. The look on their faces tells a story—a story of embarrassment, shame, confusion, even shock. They tell me, "I can't believe I struggle with this." "I thought I would just see what all the talk was about, and now I'm addicted." "I love the Lord, Sarah, and I go to Mass and youth group every Sunday. How could

I keep going back to this?" "I don't know how I got into this vicious cycle . . . or how I will ever get out." The personal stories and heart-wrenching testimonies I hear go on and on.

A girl once told me, "I don't even sin in a feminine way." I can still hear the pain in her voice, and her statement has always stuck with me. Because the struggle with pornography and masturbation has mostly been labeled a predominately male problem, countless women experience a deep interior crisis of identity, sexuality, and self-worth—all drenched in massive amounts of shame and confusion.

I remember sitting around a campfire at a retreat one night with a bunch of college women, and this topic came up. After about an hour of "real talk," one of the girls threw her hands up and said in frustration, "Why the heck isn't anyone talking about this?" I could not agree more.

Whether it was curiosity, a relationship that left you with an addiction, turning to it during a dark time in life (perhaps after a breakup), or a whole host of other reasons that brought you here, the first thing I always tell women is: "You are *not* alone." As they look back at me and say, "Really?" I hear the faintest glimmer of hope in their voices. Yes, there *is* hope. There *is* healing, and there *is* freedom from the chains that bind you. Kelsey and Everett have written from their hearts

4

and from personal testimony. In this book you will find stories, statistics, practical advice, the beautiful truth of Church teaching, and friends and guides in Kelsey and Everett, who desire to help you navigate the triggers and traps that so often ensnare people on the road to true freedom.

You are holding hope in your hands. You are not alone. Reading this book may well be the first step to replacing despair and isolation with hope and healing. I am proud of you, and I am proud of your desire to fight back. I am fighting for you and cheering you on. Please know of my love and prayers.

—Sarah Swafford

PREFACE

After graduating from college, I spent years mentoring and working with college women through a missionary organization called FOCUS. For formation and training, we spent five weeks each summer learning from top biblical scholars and professionals on various aspects of mission and the Church, in preparation of working with young men and women across the world. These classes were incredibly helpful, and I loved how much forethought and expertise were poured into each one. During my first summer training, however, I was surprised when the men and women were divided for a particular class. On the morning we were to study the virtue of chastity, men attended a class to discuss the growing issue of pornography, while women attended a class about emotional chastity (that is, how to prevent giving too much of yourself to someone too soon). These polarized classes suggested that each issue was gender specific, but that wasn't my experience.

The following year, our schedule allowed for us to discuss pornography and emotional chastity with both men and women. Attending a class on pornography intrigued me—after all, I had my own experience in this area, and had just spent the past year working with college women who had experience with it as well. However, I was quickly disappointed in the class. Although the speaker was well prepared and eloquently presented his information, every anecdote and statistic shared was only about men. He would end his stories or points made by offhandedly saying, "Oh, and this is a struggle for women too." My heart sunk.

My third summer, I knew history couldn't repeat itself. Now with two years under my belt working with young women, as well as my own experience glaring at me, something more needed to be done. Before the pornography class began, I walked up to the teacher and requested my name and contact information be given in a PowerPoint slide at the end of the presentation for any female missionary who personally struggled with pornography or masturbation and wanted to talk to someone about it. While the class went similarly as the previous year, at the very end, as requested, my name and contact information flashed across the screen. At that moment, every one of the four hundred-plus male and female missionaries turned toward me in surprise and confusion. Immediately, my face went red as I realized the daunting truth: everyone in this room now believes or knows that I have a current or past struggle with pornography or masturbation.

I was mortified.

Immediately that thought, however, was replaced with a voice. At that moment I heard Jesus say, "Kelsey, do you care?" It was then when I resolved that I didn't. I didn't care what anyone in that room thought or believed, because if someone judged me for what they assumed of my sexual purity, it would be on them. Exposing myself for the sake of my fellow female missionaries would be worth it.

And that's when it happened. Not five minutes after the class ended the flood of emails and texts began to pour in. Stories of female missionaries who had been isolated in their struggle for years were finally coming to the surface. Women who had felt so much shame and guilt in their hearts admitting to me that I was the first person they had ever told. They came to me in tears, sharing their hearts, and since they did not feel alone anymore, expressed a desire to finally be free of their addictions.

It has been said that men's struggle with pornography and masturbation is like men being held in a community prison. While still enslaved, they are at least in it together. However, for women, the struggle is like being in solitary confinement, because no one knows anyone else is in there.

That's what we have been led to believe. However, it couldn't be further from the truth. Our current culture has put our generation of women right in the middle of these struggles. The following numbers tell a very different story and are much more accurate, based on my experience.

- 76% of women ages 18–30 report that they view pornography at least once a month. This is a dramatic generational increase, as only 16% of women ages 31–49 view pornography once a month.[1]
- 78.2% of American women report having masturbated in their lifetime, and 40.8% of women reported having done so in the past month.[2]

After that third summer, I began working with young women who struggled with pornography and masturbation. I developed a proven strategy to help women through these areas and coach them on how to help others. Recognizing the importance of this issue, FOCUS invited me to teach a women-only version of the class that discussed pornography and masturbation at future summer trainings, and they invested more resources and research to better help both men and women in these areas. With this investment and greater research, I began giving talks and trainings all over the world and have walked with thousands of other women on their journey to freedom.

In these talks, one thing kept happening: while women would leave convicted they would overcome their struggle—finally knowing they weren't alone and having the steps to take to freedom—they often would fall again shortly after returning home.

A few years into working in this ministry, I met Everett Fritz. He had previously worked in youth ministry, and when the topic of sexual purity came up, he realized there wasn't a good book or resource he could recommend to help Christian Catholic men navigate these issues, one that incorporated their faith. After contacting several Catholic chastity speakers who also didn't know of a good resource, he decided to write it himself. This was the origin of *Freedom*, a book that has helped thousands of men out of the shackles of pornography and masturbation. There was only one issue with his book: it was only for men. Knowing how prevalent an issue this is for women as well, it wasn't surprising that once *Freedom* was released, requests for a female version came rushing in.

With Everett's experience and encouragement, I was excited to write a female version with him.

As you will see throughout this book, there is no quick fix to overcoming these struggles. However, there are key principles and truths we need to continually remind ourselves of in order to maintain the conviction we experience in one moment of grace. Freedom from sexual sin (or even the effects of an oversexualized culture) is a journey. This journey is easier when you have a guide, which we hope this book will be to you.

This book has three aims:

To give you advice, encouragement, and a detailed plan to avoid or overcome your struggle with pornography and/or masturbation.

To redeem your understanding of love and sexuality so you will understand what it means to love in the deepest sense of the word, and develop the will to be uncompromising in your desire for that love.

To help you develop a close, genuine relationship with Jesus Christ, who is a real person and the source of all that is pure and beautiful. We want you to know that Christ loves you beyond measure and wants to give you the grace and strength to live in freedom.

Our culture teaches us to compromise when seeking the true love that we are made for. In the modern age, women especially are being groomed to compromise more than ever before. But we are called to seek freedom in the truth of the love we were made for, and to live confidently as models for those around us.

INTRODUCTION

It was the summer before my senior year of college when I completed an internship out of state. The company I worked for was generous and paid for all three hundred interns to be housed in a local dormitory. Being typical twentysomethings, it wasn't long before many interns began coupling off, and I was no exception. Halfway through the summer, one of them caught my attention. He was smart, witty, and self-driven—very unlike many of the men I had encountered up to this point.

After spending some time together, our relationship quickly became more physical. I had recently come back to my faith and committed to living chastely, so I knew the lines I wouldn't cross and made sure to communicate them to him from the beginning. The closer he and I became, however, the blurrier those lines became. Everyone around me seemed so happy with their summer flings, so why did it matter if I crossed a line or two? I was finally in a place where I felt true independence: I had an "adult" job, was making my own living, and lived farther away from my family and friends than I ever had. Without accountability or a solid community, I let my strong ideals be completely challenged in a matter of weeks.

Eventually, one night I crossed two of my stronger lines by heavily making out and allowing this man to sleep in the same bed with me. Although we didn't have sex, I still gave him an intimate part of myself I promised I wouldn't give again until I was married. I felt sick inside. After he left the next morning, I stared at myself in the mirror. Who was this person? Had I not done this two years earlier and found no fulfillment? Had I not pulled myself out of this spiral long ago and recognized my true worth and demanded that others recognize it too? I had—and yet I had still compromised. By going further than I knew was good for me, I compromised my standards. I compromised who I was. And for what?

So I could fall into the excitement and fun of a summer fling.

So I wouldn't feel lonely.

So I would feel loved.

What I realized then was that no matter how deep my faith life had become and no matter how strong I felt in my convictions, one thing was stronger: my need to feel loved. What's beautiful about this need is that it's theological—even biblical. Our need for a relationship is good. Unfortunately, without fully understanding where it comes from, many of us are willing to compromise anything to get it, including our worth, dignity, and the beauty found within the truth of our sexuality.

This revelation helped me understand much more about our current sexual culture. Not long ago, it was commonly agreed that one should wait until marriage before having sex; that relationships and courting required upholding each other's dignity and worth at all costs; and that watching pornography and engaging in masturbation weren't healthy for dignified love. Sure, these things still happened, but culturally they weren't seen as good, or even remotely okay. However, with many shifts in our culture, these ideals are no longer standard. Today in the United States, almost everyone is open to sex before marriage (94% of women and 96% of men have sex before marriage),[3] over 40 million Americans watch pornography (76% of women and 79% of men),[4] and even more have engaged in masturbation (78.2% of women, 91.8% of men).[5] But how did this happen?

Supply and Demand

Supply is the amount of something available, and demand is the amount that something is desired. Let's say we have fifty men and fifty women. Originally, all fifty women had a certain standard (or cost) for what kind of love they were worth in a relationship and what they required from men who wanted to pursue them. A man had to properly court her: ask permission from her parents, take her on many well-planned dates, and wait patiently before the relationship became remotely physical. And yes, most often, waited for sex until marriage. Eventually, however, some women were okay with not waiting until marriage for sex, so men started pursuing them more (women lowered their standards, or their "cost"). These women were now receiving the "love" they desperately desired to feel. As women with lower standards became more common, competition struck again. Next, someone said, "All men have to do is tell me they love me, and I will have sex with them." Next, "All you have to do is call me your girlfriend." Then, "All you need to do is take me out for a nice dinner." Until finally, "All you need to do is swipe right."

Women began compromising. Women began changing their ideals for the supply of a "committed, loving relationship" by lowering their standards until men didn't need to do much of anything.

Maybe you're thinking, "Kelsey, it's not compromising if it's their choice. There are tons of women who choose a casual relationship or sexual lifestyle and that is their right." And you would be correct; it is their decision. However, what led them to make that "choice" in the first place? And how is that lifestyle working out for them? Our current "sexually free" culture claims to empower women, and yet, this is exactly what has led us to a culture of divorce, physical and sexual abuse, and women's dissatisfaction in their relationships. Women may compromise in the name of "sexual freedom" or self-expression, but this doesn't change the effect it has on our society as a whole. Archbishop Fulton Sheen once said, "To a great extent the level of any civilization is the level of its womanhood. When a man loves a woman, he has to become worthy of her. The higher her virtue, the nobler her character, the more devoted she is to truth, justice, goodness, the more a man has to aspire to be worthy of her. The history of civilization could be written in terms of the level of its women."[6]

As women, we need to start with ourselves and demand more. We need to stand up alongside one another and raise the standard of what we expect from others and the world. We must be uncompromising in who we are, the standards we hold for ourselves and others, and the truth and beauty we have been bestowed in Jesus Christ.

As you will see in this book, pornography and masturbation are two aspects of how women have been targeted to compromise, especially in recent years. By seeking freedom from pornography and masturbation, by living an uncompromised life dedicated to living beyond what our culture tells us will make us happy, and by actually choosing what has been proven to provide joy, strength, and fulfillment for women, we can live the lives God intended when he looked at his creation and said boldly, "It is very good" (Gen. 1:31).

CHAPTER 1

My Story

I was twelve. I had no name for it and didn't even know it existed. Like many preteens, I had already fallen victim to the laundry list of popular movies involving crude humor and sexually explicit content. While flipping through television stations over the years, I stumbled upon movies in which I saw men and women engaging in a behavior I had never encountered before. Even though I knew about sex, this was different. On-screen, it was displayed as normal and good, and I was intrigued. One evening, I decided to see what all the hype was about.

The first time I masturbated, it was a result of mere curiosity. There was no ill intention, no painful wounds dredged up from my past, and certainly no knowledge of how it would affect me. As I began "testing" out this new behavior, I noticed it calmed me down and often made me forget anything difficult or painful I was going through at the time (at least for a moment). As I transitioned into the more demanding world of high school, this behavior grew to be my reliable companion during times of academic pressure, heartache, and emotional distress caused by family, friendships, boys, work, or school.

During the same time, I left my Catholic faith and became agnostic after witnessing many self-proclaimed Christians bring pain and suffering into the world. I instead considered myself a woman of reason and science. I decided to live by a personal code of morals, which I thought would lead me to "ultimate happiness." Through this rational approach, I continued to learn about human sexuality and masturbation and understood it to be a natural and healthy release without the risks of STDs or pregnancy. By the time I graduated high school, it had become a daily habit. At the time, I would never have said I had an addiction. After all, I was engaging in masturbation as my free choice!

I came back into the Catholic Church before my senior year of high school, and even though I learned about the teachings of chastity, pornography and masturbation were never brought up. In my mind, since I wasn't having sex, I was simply finding a healthier alternative.

"I have a problem."
When I got to college, my behavior continued. Schedule changes, dorm life, and no longer having the seclusion of my own room decreased the frequency; however, I

would take the opportunity of being home alone to get "my fix." As I did this, I recalled scenes in movies or created fantasies in my head to get the same release I had gotten in high school. I occasionally searched online for kissing scenes in popular movies, and eventually, romantic sex scenes. I justified the behavior by telling myself it was harmless since I wasn't explicitly watching X-rated content from a "pornographic" site.

By the time I was a junior, however, I was further along in my faith. I had encountered Jesus Christ in a profound way and my relationship with him began changing the way I lived. I stopped drinking underage and committed to never get drunk or make out with random guys at parties. A missionary I encountered at the time was teaching me how to develop a prayer life and challenged me to give everything to Christ. During these years, it was always in the back of my mind that my personal chastity wasn't okay by Christian Catholic standards, but since I wasn't "hurting anyone" and I definitely "wasn't addicted," the Church had (obviously) gotten their stance on this one wrong.

That same year of college, I learned that a guy friend of mine was giving up masturbation for Lent. If masturbation was wrong, I knew I couldn't count it as a fast during Lent, but his idea left me curious. After all, I was convinced I could stop whenever I wanted, so what would be the harm? I decided to put it to the test and stop masturbating during Lent to prove that I was in control of my behavior. If I was correct and could do it easily, I resolved it was okay to continue my behavior after Lent at my discretion.

The first two weeks were easy. Life was normal, and I never even thought about masturbation as an option. I knew I was right about this whole "addiction thing" anyway. By week three, however, I noticed it popping into my mind, so I started planning more activities to be out of the house and around people. One month in, it was all I could think about. Whether it was a movie scene or fantasy coming to mind, or just the urge in my body growing, I couldn't seem to shake it. I was looking at men in my life and on-screen differently and became frustrated. What was going on? How did I get here? Was I *not* in control of my behavior? Had masturbation been affecting me like this all this time?

I was shocked, ashamed, and hurt by my lies that had made their way so deep into my heart. I remembered the freedom and joy I experienced during the first two weeks of Lent and compared it to how I felt now. This feeling consumed my whole life, and I began to see how much I had become a slave to this habit. How could this happen without me noticing? The next morning, I walked straight up to a priest and made my first confession that included masturbation. I went through every step of my story and cried the whole time. Walking away from that confession was incredible. At that moment, I discovered a new lightness and freedom that words can't describe.

Now, I wish I could end the story right there. Tell you "and that's my story. From there, I was cleansed of my sin and never again fell into the throes of masturbation or pornography."

But that would be a lie.

In reality, this is where my story begins. The road to freedom starts with recognizing that you are not in control, and you need Jesus Christ to bring you out of your addiction. After all, we were not made to live in slavery, we were made to experience and live in true, authentic freedom.

The Journey Ahead

Your story may be similar to mine, or you may not be able to relate. Regardless of whether you have shame in your life related to sexual impurity or you have no experience, I encourage you to keep reading.

Throughout this book, practical steps will be provided to put you on the path to freedom. If you have pornography or masturbation issues in your life, or you have a history of sexual activity with a partner, the first step is acknowledging where you struggle. Take heart—our God is merciful and loving. These habits are not the story of your life, rather God's glory in guiding you out of these addictions and into his arms.

If you don't have these issues in your past, praise God! There is still a tremendous amount of advice for you in this book. Sexual addiction doesn't happen overnight. Rather, it happens as the world erodes our understanding of truth, causing us to compromise our deepest convictions in return for a promise of something "more valuable." The trade is never fair, as the world's promises always fail to deliver.

The only person who always delivers on his promises is God. As we will see in the next chapter, he has a plan for love in your life, and that plan was perfect from the beginning.

Reflection Questions

1. What about Kelsey's story stands out to you?
2. How have you been affected by pornography or our oversexualized culture throughout your life?
3. Is pornography or masturbation something you have struggled with?
4. What do you hope to get out of reading this book?
5. Do you believe true freedom is possible for you?

CHAPTER 2

God's Plan for Love and Sex

When many people think of what the Church has to say about sex, they see a big sign flashing NO! That is a fair opinion when you consider that these are the messages most people have heard from people representing the Church:

NO sex before marriage!
NO kissing, touching, or intimacy of any sort!
NO masturbation!
NO pornography!
If you do any of these things, you will get pregnant
    or get STDs and bad things will happen to you!
You will go to hell if you break the rules!

However, this is a misrepresentation of the true teaching of the Church about our sexuality. If people truly knew God and the Church's view of sexuality, they would be surprised. The fullness of its teaching on sexuality is not a *no* to its abuses, but a resounding *YES* to the fundamental goodness of this God-given gift. To understand the true meaning of our sexuality, we need to go back to the beginning.

Genesis

On the sixth day, "God created man in his own image . . . male and female he created them . . . and he said to them, 'Be fruitful and multiply'" (Gen. 1:27–28). These verses are countercultural, as they speak to two profound elements of creation: that it wasn't complete until there were two distinct sexes, and that once they were created, the first thing God commanded was for man and woman to consummate and procreate.

God explains the reason for this in the next chapter: "The Lord God said: 'It is not good for man to be alone. I will make a suitable partner for him'" (Gen. 2:18). After creating all the living creatures in the world, God is still not satisfied until he creates woman. Once he creates woman to be a partner for Adam, God brings her to Adam, to which Adam responds, "At last, this one is bone of my bones and flesh of my flesh . . . That is why a man leaves his father and mother and clings to his wife, and the two of them become one flesh" (Gen. 2:21–24). Here, God unites man and woman in a supernatural covenant between them and

God himself. This is the first account of marriage we have, and it's from our very origin!

Pope Saint John Paul II tells us that "the fundamental fact of human existence at every stage of its history is that God 'created them male and female.'"[7] Man and woman were created for love, and "in the mystery of [this] creation, man and woman [become] a mutual gift."[8] Jesus reminds us of this life-altering aspect of marriage in the Gospel of Matthew by stating, "They are no longer two but one. Therefore, what God has joined together, let no one separate" (Matt. 19:6).

Unfortunately, this understanding of marriage as a mutual gift and belief in a lifelong covenant is rarely seen in our culture today. Almost 50% of marriages in the United States end in divorce or separation, and the average length of time in a first marriage that ends in divorce is only eight years.[9] However, even though divorce is now a common experience, our hearts yearn for something much different. Seeing an elderly couple hold hands, sneak a kiss, or simply sitting together affects us in an unexplainable way. It's because this type of love and lifelong commitment is what our hearts and souls are made for, even if the rest of the world has forgotten.

Love, Sex, and Marriage

The greatest desire of any human person (either female and male) is to give and receive love. God created sex to speak the language of this true "life-giving" love.

Love requires willing the good of the other. The love between any two people—husbands and wives, mothers and their children, best friends at school—demands selflessness, sacrifice, and lots of compassion. For example, I love my daughter, but there was one night when she woke up screaming every hour because she didn't feel well. I had an important presentation at work the next day and I needed to be on my A-game. I did not harbor warm feelings for her at that moment; however, I did what was good for her. I got out of bed, comforted her in her illness, fed her multiple times throughout the night, and gave her medicine to make her feel better. I love my daughter, and love required me to disregard my comfort and physical desire for sleep, as well as my concerns about work, and to do what was best for her.

If sex speaks a language of love, then it would make sense that the love communicated by it is about more than just physical pleasure. There must be a deeper message communicated in the sexual relations between a man and a woman.

Like all languages, the "language" of sex has certain elements for it to be properly ordered, which in this case were written by the Divine Author himself. What is needed for properly expressing this language of love through sex?

Sex is designed to be *freely given*. God does not desire for anyone to be forced into a sexual relationship. Both man and woman should come together of their own free will, without external or internal coercion.

Sex is designed to be *total*, entailing a complete gift of self. In the act of sexual intercourse, the man and woman give their entire bodies and persons to one another. They hold nothing back. They present a total self-gift of love.

Sex is designed to be *faithful*. The language of sex says, "I give myself to you and no one else." This is an exclusive relationship.

Sex is designed to be *fruitful*, uniting the couple in a deep bond of love that is ordered toward the procreation of new life.

So why is it so important to understand God's plan for sex and what He wants to be communicated by it? The language of freely given, total, faithful, and fruitful love is expressed in the promises and vows that two Christians make in the sacrament of matrimony. When my husband and I were married, we made three essential promises: we freely consented to enter marriage; we acknowledged marriage as an indissoluble union of mutual love and respect; and we were prepared to welcome children and bring them up in the Catholic faith. Then we exchanged vows that we would be faithful to one another in good times and in bad, in sickness and in health, until death do us part.

These were our promises and vows. Only after making these was it right for us to consummate our marital union with our bodies, through the marital embrace that expresses this language of exclusive, lifelong love and commitment.

Our Role in the Trinity

The beauty of this love between a man and a woman can also be seen within God himself, the Trinity. As we saw in Genesis, we were made in the "image and likeness" of God. But have you ever asked yourself what that means? God is three Persons in one—the Father, Son, and Holy Spirit. Therefore, God at his core is a relationship. When people say, "God is Love," it can be taken literally. God is a being who is an eternal exchange of love, as three Persons in one. If you are a visual person, the diagram below will help demonstrate this exchange:

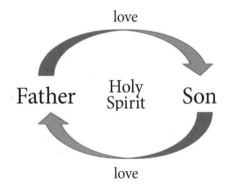

As the Father freely and wholly loves and gives himself to his son, Jesus, Jesus receives this love from the Father. Jesus then gives himself back to the Father as a free gift of himself. The Holy Spirit proceeds from this exchange of giving and receiving complete love between the Father and Son.

So if the previous diagram articulates the Trinity and God's full identity that we were made in the image and likeness of, then God would have designed a way for us to partake in this eternal exchange of love as well. From the perspective of a relationship with Jesus, we can see this demonstrated below:

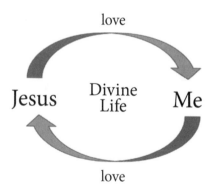

As Jesus gave himself fully and freely for our sake at his Passion on the Cross, our first role is to receive this love and gift of his sacrifice. Only by receiving this love can we, in turn, give ourselves freely back in love to Jesus. Through this receiving and giving exchange of love comes our participation in the Divine Life. We partake in Trinitarian love.

While all baptized Christians are called to live out their identity in the Trinity as shown in the previous diagram (priests and religious even more so through their consecration and vows), some are also called to live out this trinitarian exchange of love through holy matrimony. This is demonstrated below:

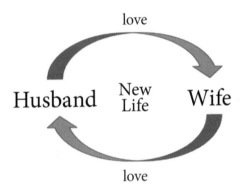

As we can see, a husband's first role is to give himself fully to his wife just as Jesus did for the Church (Eph. 5:25). The wife's first role then is to receive this love and return it to her husband as a full gift of self. From this exchange, the possibility of new life (a baby) is created.

As the Creator of sex, God is the embodiment of love. He desired more from the gift of our sexuality.

He desired for men to give love and security within our sexuality and for women to receive the gift of life and love within her own body.

Everything in us is made for this type of exchange. Just look at our biology. Women's bodies are made as human tabernacles that have the capacity first to receive her spouse before having the potential to carry a God-infused soul inside of her womb. Miraculous. Even women who struggle with infertility experience this full receptivity of her spouse and potential for new life, as all things are possible with God—just look at Sarah conceiving Isaac in her old age (Gen. 17–21). What this means, however, is that while everything in us is made for this type of life-giving exchange, it also means we may look for it in the wrong places. When pornography and masturbation are introduced into this equation, the diagram becomes disconnected:

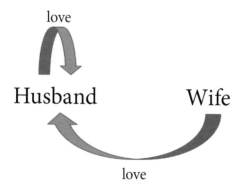

love

Husband   Wife

love

love

Wife

Husband

love

When one or both partners decide to experience this sexual union on their own, they cut off their ability to be a full gift of self to their spouse or anyone else. These actions break their commitment to be faithful and fruitful within their relationship. Once they take this exchange of giving and receiving love onto themselves, they are no longer able to enter into a trinitarian relationship—which is what they were made for. They compromise for a lesser "love," and will ultimately end up unsatisfied and unfulfilled.

God's Plan vs. the World's Idea

Sex in our culture involves no permanent commitment and seeks self-gratification and pleasure as the highest goals. In the case of masturbation and pornography, there isn't even a real person with whom we communicate love. It turns our expression of sexuality entirely inward, and our interest is only in "fulfilling" our appetites and desires. Even in the context of a dating relationship between two people who may love each other, sex does not communicate true love, because the individuals have yet to commit to a lifelong, exclusive vow to be a mutual gift for the other. Rather than expressing truth, sex between two such people is acting out a lie. By its very nature, a lie cannot give genuine satisfaction. This has even been proven. Research to determine which demographic has the most satisfying sex lives shows it is devout Catholic married couples. Not only do they have more fulfilling sexual relations, but they are also intimate more often![10]

The growing onslaught of a variety of sex-tips articles, scenarios, toys, and so on that are intended to "spice up your sex life" makes it safe to say that there is a lot of dissatisfaction out there. There is something within our hearts that is not being fulfilled, and therefore we seek fulfillment by trying to gratify ourselves through progressive sexual expressions and immorality. But void of real love, no form of sexual arousal can fulfill our deepest desires.

I believe it is this yearning for deeper meaning and intimacy that explains why so many women are drawn to pornography and masturbation. Without knowing and living the purpose and meaning for sex, we fall for the cheapest imitation. Only by constantly reminding ourselves of the true love we were made for, the love only found within the beauty and Divine Life of the

Trinity, can we begin to remove the shackles that come with pornography and masturbation.

You may wonder if men exist who wish to live out the virtues of chastity and authentic love. These men absolutely exist! But there is something you should know about these men: they don't date women who compromise. This isn't to say that real men won't date a woman who has made mistakes. Rather, the kind of man who will commit to a life of communicating God's love in a relationship is attracted to uncompromising virtue. He is looking for a woman who shares his convictions. To find this type of man, put yourself in places and communities of friends that support and encourage these ideals.

Reflection Questions

1. Before reading this chapter, what was your understanding of how the Church viewed sex and marriage?
2. Compare and contrast your perception of Church teaching on sexuality with what was articulated in this chapter. What was different?
3. What do you think of God's design for sex to be freely given, total self-gift, faithful, and fruitful in giving life (physical and spiritual) to another? What do you think your friends would think of this?

4. We are made in the image and likeness of God, and God is a communion of Persons, the Holy Trinity. How does this concept help you to understand your identity?
5. John Paul II said that "only the chaste man and chaste woman are capable of true love."[11] What do you think he meant by that?

CHAPTER 3

How You Got
Hooked . . .

Many people debate what pornography is or isn't. In today's culture, it has permeated so many channels that it's almost impossible to entirely avoid it. Several experts say that the average age of first exposure is somewhere between nine and eleven years old. Most often, the first exposure is unintentional, whether by a friend or family member, or by stumbling upon it accidentally during an internet search.

The Catechism of the Catholic Church defines pornography as "removing real or simulated sexual acts from the intimacy of the partners, to display them deliberately to third parties."[12] This broad definition could apply to a multitude of outlets. It's important to recognize pornography does not only consist of explicit X-rated films or magazines found at your local "adult store." If we use the *Catechism*'s definition, thousands of top box-office films, bestselling books, prime-time television shows, everyday commercials, billboards, music videos, popular magazine covers/main content, video games, websites, applications on your phone, and many other similar things all include pornography.

We have divided pornography into two basic categories: explicit and implicit. Explicit pornography is the more commonly known version—graphic visual and/or written X-rated content. Implicit pornography is content that displays more hidden or assumed sexual intimacy of parties, visually and/or written, intentionally to be used for personal arousal.

The last part of the "implicit" definition includes an important distinction. While pornography may be everywhere in today's culture, women may not always transition into intentionally seeking it out or using implicit pornographic material for their sexual pleasure (fantasies or acting out through masturbation). Therefore, when discussing an addiction or attachment to implicit pornography, we are referring to the deliberate seeking out or use for personal arousal.

It was this type of implicit pornography I slowly became addicted to without realizing it. This kind of pornography can be even more dangerous, as it's more widely accepted and promoted in our society. Therefore, seeking it out can easily be justified. It can also be a gateway or stumbling block for those trying to overcome an addiction to explicit pornography.

Women often have a beautiful gift for creating stories in our minds. Think back to times playing with baby dolls as a child, fascination with Barbie, or the ability to role-play "house" for hours on end. While women can become just as easily addicted to explicit pornography, they don't always seek graphic, X-rated content for visual stimulation of sexual pleasure. Whether it's explicit or implicit, women often concentrate on the story behind pornographic content: the relationship between two people or the suggested sexual tension can be enough for a woman to create an elaborate scenario in her mind to engage in sexual fantasies and/or masturbation later on. Over time, this subtle collection of scenes or story lines from TV shows or movies can build to even greater fantasies without ever recognizing the potential risk of these fantasies growing into a pornography addiction.

Due to our brain's neural connections, it can take multiple years to forget images or scenes of pornography. Depending on the length of time you have built up these connections, it could take much longer than you might expect. No matter where you are in your journey toward purity, chances are, if given one minute to write down as many sex scenes/scenarios you can remember from everyday mediums, you could probably come up with a lengthy list.

Now, you may be thinking, "Okay, Kelsey, although I have seen sex portrayed in movies, television, and advertisements, I don't have a pornography addiction!" And you may be right. Watching or reading some of the previously mentioned outlets doesn't automatically mean you have an addiction; however, when adding up the amount of sexual content we have been exposed to, it's no wonder that rates of men and women with pornography and masturbation habits are skyrocketing. The more frequently we fill ourselves with these simulated accounts of sex, the more we are affected. If you struggle with any kind of pornography or masturbation, it's essential to reflect on what kind of content you are continually and intentionally seeking out. No matter your sexual habits, you should remove all potentially dangerous sexual content from your life.

A good litmus test is to ask yourself, "If I was watching this with my parents or with my grandmother in the room, would I feel uncomfortable?" If the answer is yes, it's most likely not appropriate for us either.

Defining the Issue: Masturbation

Next, let's consider masturbation. The *Catechism* defines masturbation as "the deliberate stimulation of the genital organs to derive sexual pleasure."[13] I once believed and have had several women tell me that it only counts as masturbation if you reach orgasm. However, from the *Catechism*'s definition, we can see this isn't the case. Any intentional sexual stimulation of your genitalia can be harmful to you, as that is all it takes to begin an addiction. This stimulation can be through the use of devices or not, but it must be intentional.

While data demonstrates an ever-growing rate of women addicted to pornography, women's engagement in masturbation has been high for quite some time (78.2% of women have reported having masturbated in the past).[14] Going back to our understanding of implicit pornography, many women can have an addiction to masturbation without ever seeing an X-rated film.

Someone's first exposure to masturbation can occur through learning from a friend or another outlet similar to pornography. However, many women can't remember their first exposure. Children as early as two years old may begin stimulating themselves out of curiosity or a biological urge. If this habit is not appropriately addressed early on, the practice can become imprinted in the brain through the frequent release of dopamine and oxytocin. At this age of innocence, the act isn't culpable, and therefore should be without shame. However, depending on the frequency and longevity of this ingrained habit, even once women learn what they are doing is masturbation and desire to stop, they often struggle to overcome their habit.

It's also important to note that if you have a past of pornography or masturbation addiction, the threshold of what you can watch or read may be lower than it is for others. It's okay that you may not be able to handle watching something that someone else doesn't even see could be tempting. During my road to freedom from my sexual addictions, I remember watching an awards show performance in which one of the artists acted in a sexually suggestive way. I immediately closed my eyes and wished I could take back the past five seconds. While the rest of my roommates agreed it was an appalling display of sexuality on TV, I admitted to them that the scene brought arousal to me and I felt ashamed. Although they didn't have the same response, we all committed to better protect each other from the content we allowed to surround us.

No matter where your threshold is, we never know where someone else may be with their sexual addiction, so it is important to protect our sisters as much as possible. If you have or currently struggle with pornography or masturbation, there is no shame in protecting your mind and heart from certain images or stories by saying no to watching a movie or TV show with a group of friends. You may be the strength and witness a fellow sister may need to overcome her struggle as well.

Justification

I often hear from women that they know they shouldn't watch pornography or engage in masturbation, yet they can't seem to stop. If we know things like pornography, masturbation, or other sexual acts can be harmful to ourselves and our relationships, why do we still fall into the trap?

To better understand this, let's make a comparison to something less controversial, such as gossiping. When talking with a group of women, I have begun to address the topic of pornography or masturbation by asking the following:

"Who here thinks we should gossip, that it is a good thing to do?"

No one raises her hand.

"Okay, who here has ever gossiped?"

All hands slowly lift into the air.

"So why do we do this if no one thinks we should? What do we gain? Meaning, what benefits could come from us gossiping?"

Answers vary, but typically, these are some of them:

- Less stress due to the release of a burdening secret or story
- Increased bond in friendship with the person they are sharing the story with
- Gained knowledge about people in their life
- Opportunity to pray for someone, or sympathize greater with them
- Saves time from having to discover the information on their own

- Potential to feel better about their own life or situation

Based on all these things, if God truly wants good things for us, gossiping sounds great! Less stress, deeper friendships, more knowledge, and a potential opportunity to pray or feel better about your own life? God would want that for us, right?

This is the problem: we are so accustomed to rationalizing our actions in a matter of seconds that we don't realize we are doing it. Although we may know something could be "wrong," it is easy to quickly give in to the desire to justify our actions, especially if we know there are potential good outcomes as well. The same thing happens internally when we battle the temptation of pornography or masturbation.

Recall the story of our creation: Adam and Eve were given one rule at the beginning: not to eat of the tree of knowledge in the Garden. The consequence if they didn't follow this rule? Death.

This seems pretty cut and dry. Nevertheless, we see Eve fall prey to the Devil's lies and she chooses to eat of the fruit anyway.

But is this the whole story?

Just before eating the fruit, Eve notices that the tree is good for nourishment, pleasing to the eyes, and would give her wisdom of good and bad. These were good things: she sees goodness, beauty, and truth within the tree. Therefore, her choice to eat of the fruit was a distortion of the truth. Her intention to seek good things resulted in her receiving something devastatingly harmful. We see this distortion of truth played out in many ways in our own lives.

Even if we don't verbalize the "benefits" we receive from pornography or masturbation, our body goes ahead to think on our behalf. Just like other drugs, it is proven that through engaging in these things, stress levels temporarily decrease, dopamine (the good-feeling chemical) is released in our brain, and oxytocin (the relationship connection hormone) is released, making us forget any feeling of loneliness or isolation. It sounds like a dream come true! These benefits allow us to justify our behavior. No matter how deep our faith life is, or how strong our convictions about the harms of pornography and masturbation are, all of us can become susceptible to the following justifications:

"Only this once"

Just like when Eve ate of the fruit, many consequences come from these temporary chemical "fixes." Our brain is not meant to process the artificially stimulated release of these chemicals. As you continue to watch pornography or engage in masturbation, you will need to increase the frequency or go more extreme in these things to receive the same chemical benefits. While it may initially be a "one-time thing," you will begin to notice that engaging even just once will increase your temptation the next time, as well as lower your inhibitions to stay strong in the face of that temptation.

"I'm not hurting anyone"

When I began engaging in masturbation, I saw it as a great solution to the sexual urges that were increasing in my body. After listening to Crystalina Evert's chastity talk in high school, I learned the harms of having sex before marriage and decided to wait to have sex until marriage. However, although I knew that sex before marriage created bonds with men who weren't my husband and that sex was meant to be a full gift of self only able to be achieved in the lifelong commitment and sacrament of marriage, those reasons didn't apply to giving yourself personal sexual pleasure. Through masturbation, I thought, I wasn't attaching myself unhealthily to any man, nor was I giving a full gift of myself without commitment. It was strictly physical and I was the only one involved.

But that's not the case.

While it may not be as obvious, much of the harm of pornography and masturbation is that you are using another during it. The damage is twofold:

First, when watching pornography, you are visually stripping the actors of their human dignity, using their sexuality and God-created bodies for your pleasure. You do not know them and certainly don't have any commitment to selflessly will their good. Instead, you are exploiting their bodies and their sexuality. Pornography displays a person's sexuality without their full personhood and worth being a part of the equation. Even in masturbation, you are pulling to mind images or scenes of individuals from memory to use for the same reason.

Secondly, you are not fully loving your future spouse (and if you are called to single or religious life, God and the Church). Our human sexuality is designed by God for our future spouse alone. As explained in the last chapter, love requires us to present our sexuality as a free and full gift of self in a lifelong commitment to each other. Sexuality is ordered toward creating life and unity within marriage. Pornography and masturbation directly remove both of those purposes. Furthermore, the greater your frequency or level of engagement in pornography and masturbation, the greater you are desensitized to sex in general. Many marriages suffer from a dissatisfied sex life or inability to perform largely because one or both spouse's previous or current engagement in these harmful avenues.[15]

"The Church is wrong"

I once talked with a young woman who told me she received a sex toy as a gift from her mother on her sixteenth birthday. According to her mother, a woman needs to learn about her sexuality through "safe experimenting" because experimentation empowers a woman to take control of her sexuality. While I was talking with this young woman, she asked if the Catholic Church has wrongly guilted people into thinking there is something wrong with pornography and masturbation when it is actually liberating and very beneficial to women. In listening to her question, my heart broke inside. In a society that not only accepts pornography and masturbation but has parents feeding it to their children, it is an increasingly difficult battle. Many things became common in our culture before we learned that they harm us and need to be regulated or avoided entirely (smoking, taking certain medications, eating foods with heavy chemicals or pesticides, etc.).

While the Church does warn us of the harms of pornography and masturbation from a spiritual and eternal perspective, it's equally important to look at the scientific and empirical evidence that demonstrates the harms of these things as well. Simply looking at the changes in brain chemistry, the increase in depression or anxiety disorders, or decreased sexual satisfaction in current and future relationships should be enough to show us that pornography and masturbation do not lend themselves to "liberation" or "empowerment."[16] These secular reports and data all show the same thing: the more that men and women consume pornography or engage in masturbation, the more distorted their minds, relationships, and personal sexual understanding becomes.

Finding Healing

Regardless of what justification you have used in the past, or where your addiction currently stands, it's important not to fall into despair.

Our oversexualized culture exposed you to explicit or implicit pornography (likely at a young age) and you have been conditioned by our culture to reduce yourself to an object to be used in the pursuit of sexual gratification.

The path to freedom is a journey and it will take time and endurance to reach your destination. The good news is that you will not be walking that path alone. God created you to be loved wholly and freely, and if you allow him, he will walk with you on the journey. The next step is to acknowledge the wounds that have led to addiction so you can present them to the Divine Healer. Living out uncompromising purity can be difficult if you go it alone, but Christ can heal your wounds and set you on the path to the life-giving love he created you for. In the next chapter, we will walk you through what this looks like.

Reflection Questions

1. What do you think of the *Catechism*'s definitions of pornography and masturbation? How do they differ from your understanding?

2. What aspects of our oversexualized culture could potentially be harmful to someone trying to experience freedom from pornography or masturbation?

3. Have you ever used one of the justifications listed in this chapter for your sexual behavior? Have you used a different one?

4. What have you heard from others regarding the "benefits" of pornography and masturbation?

5. How would you best address these comments or mentality?

CHAPTER 4

Hope in Healing

Several years into working on becoming free of my addiction, in a moment of weakness and temptation, I fell again into the sin of masturbation. At this point, I had already started helping several other women overcome their addictions and was training missionaries on how to help themselves and the women they worked with in ministry. Through all this, I thought I should be over these struggles by now. I had fallen previously in my journey toward freedom, but this time was different. I remember very clearly choosing to give in to temptation, and afterward, I felt indifferent.

I was overcome with the thought that this struggle was too hard, and I was only human. Instead of the usual frustration and guilt I felt after falling, I was met with complacency and assumed total freedom from these things must not be something I could achieve. I purposefully did not go to the sacrament of confession, avoided my accountability partner, and continued to attend daily Mass and receive the

Eucharist in sin. I ignored Jesus in prayer and went on "spiritual autopilot."

It wasn't that I didn't want freedom or the full healing of these struggles in my life, but I didn't know what else I was missing. I remember thinking that if someone who was as devoted to her prayer life, the sacraments, and her daily relationship with Christ couldn't choose Jesus over this sin, then she didn't deserve to be forgiven. *I* didn't deserve to be forgiven.

Only You

During this internal battle, I went on a retreat. With Good Friday approaching, the talks revolved around Jesus' Crucifixion and death, and one of the speakers brought up something Jesus said at the end of his Passion. Just when Jesus was nailed and lifted onto the Cross, he called out, "Father, forgive them for they know not what they do" (Luke 24:34). It was at this time of the Crucifixion when nearly all of Jesus' followers had scattered and he was left with those who were bitter, hostile, and resentful, calling him names, spitting at him, and stripping him of every last shred of dignity. Yet Jesus chose this as the moment to ask his Father to forgive them.

Reflecting on this, I realized there is nothing we could do in our lives that is worse than brutally attacking and killing the Son of God. We already did this, and we have been forgiven for it. It was this very act of brutality that allowed Christ to save all of us from our sins. God knew our hearts so well that he chose the moment when humanity was at its worst to declare forgiveness for all.

I took this into prayer and wrestled with God about why he would do it this way. I looked up at a crucifix and was confronted with my previous years of struggle to break free of my sexual addictions. All of the hurt, pain, and guilt came rushing down like a waterfall and I begged God to show me why I was worthy of forgiveness. As I peered up at him through my tears, I felt Jesus calling out to my heart. It was slightly above a whisper, but I heard him say, "You are my daughter." He continued, "and I would do it all over again, even if it was only for you."

I lost it. I've been told before that Jesus would have been crucified for just one soul, but for him to say that the soul was mine was overwhelming. Christ would have gone through every moment of the pain and suffering he endured leading up to and on the Cross if it was only me . . . or only you . . . who needed saving.

I had been holding on so tightly to the fact that I needed to be worthy of God's forgiveness, instead of engaging the very relationship that Jesus came to restore. While I thought I was relying on Christ to help me overcome my addiction, I was trying to achieve self-control through *my* conviction and strength. The Devil knew this and knew the best way to keep me from receiving healing and total freedom was to keep me from understanding Jesus' love for me, and therefore, his saving power of forgiveness.

We Need a Savior

To be a Christian means to acknowledge we need a Savior. When we surrender our lives to Christ and allow him to rescue us from bondage to sin, we learn to rely on the grace the Holy Spirit bestows upon us. Grace is God's very life working within us, "the free and undeserved help that God gives us to respond to his call to become children of God" (CCC 1996). When we learn to follow him, we learn to rely on his grace. When we receive the sacraments, when we pray for God's grace, and when we follow Jesus day by day, we rely on his grace. The grace of God transforms us from the inside out, and the hardest work of converting our hearts and minds is done by God himself.

If our goal was merely to stop sexual sin, you might be able to do that with a few exercises in self-control or discipline. But that isn't our end goal. Our goal is total freedom. Our goal is to become uncompromising in our pursuit of the love we are created for. This isn't possible without a relationship with Jesus Christ. Jesus—who walked the earth two thousand years ago, is love in the flesh. Every teaching he gave describes God as Love, and it is that loving relationship we ultimately desire.

Every person is in a different place on their faith journey. You may know nothing of Jesus. You may know a lot about Jesus. But do you have a close relationship with him? Consider something that Saint Teresa of Calcutta wrote to all of the Missionaries of Charity:

"I worry some of you still have not really met Jesus—one to one—you and Jesus alone. We may spend time in chapel—but have you seen with the eyes of your soul how he looks at you with love? Do you really know the living Jesus—not from books but from being with him in your heart? Have you heard the loving words he speaks to you? Ask for the grace, he is longing to give it."[17]

Mother Teresa wrote this to women who have given everything to follow Christ through living in poverty, chastity, and obedience. She worried that some of them still hadn't met Christ, at least not in a personal manner. Saying no to counterfeits of love becomes much easier when you live and remain in the love of Jesus Christ. The reason I encourage you to be uncompromising is that I do not want you to compromise on love. Real love is what you deserve, and it is only in Jesus

Christ and with those who live by his example that you will find the love you are looking for.

Christ the Healer

Why is it that women compromise on love? Because we are human and humans are wounded. Deep down we have stopped believing it is possible to be loved the way our heart desires. We forget our identity in Jesus Christ and often try to escape the feeling of being "unloved" in past or current experiences by seeking consolation wherever we can find it. This is a wound, and every time the pain surfaces, we can fall into the sin of masturbation, pornography, and empty or sometimes even abusive relationships. But no matter how deep the wound, Christ can fully restore us.

I have often wondered what it is like for Christ to speak one word and miraculously heal someone. How can words have such an impact on someone's life that they cause the impossible to happen? Jesus spoke and Lazarus came back to life. Jesus spoke and the deaf heard. God speaks at the beginning of time and the world comes into existence. And there are countless other times when all God has to do is speak and a person is healed.

However, sometimes God chooses to heal in a different manner. For example, in the Gospel of Mark, people bring a blind man to Jesus and beg the Lord to touch him. After doing so, Jesus asks him, "Do you see anything?" The man looked up and said, "I see men; but they look like trees, walking." Again he laid his hands upon the man's eyes, and only then was his vision fully restored (Mark 8:22–26). It's peculiar that the God who spoke creation into existence seemed to need two attempts to heal this man. But nothing is accidental with God. Perhaps he wanted to show us that healing is often more a process than a declaration. Therefore, do not lose heart as God completes the work he began in you (Phil. 1:6).

Begin with Prayer

If you are journeying through sexual impurity to a life of freedom and uncompromising love, the starting point is prayer. Pray every day, for two intentions. First, that you would know intimately the love of Jesus Christ. Second, that you would know and identify your wounds. When you identify a wound, present it to Christ and pray that he speaks truth and love into the lies, sins, and hurt.

Have no false expectations: the journey to freedom will be difficult. But the first step doesn't have to be. The first step is giving Jesus permission to lead you. If you are willing to begin the journey, then pray the following prayer:

Jesus, I pray that you would take me by the hand and lead me to freedom from sexual impurity.

I pray that I may know you intimately, that you would reveal yourself in my life. I pray that I may know you better and grow closer to you every day. Jesus, I know that the journey will be difficult, and I ask that you will strengthen me for it. Jesus, I pray that you will bring to light my wounds that are attached to sexual impurity and that you will bring healing to those wounds. I pray that you will bring relationships into my life that will support my commitment to chastity. I ask you to remove relationships that pull me away from you. I pray that you will guide me through temptation and protect me from evil and selfishness. Jesus, be my teacher. Teach me to love. Teach me to pray. Teach me to love like you—to be the woman you created me to be. Should I struggle, carry me through that struggle. Should I fall, have mercy on me and lead me back to you. Guide my intentions, desires, and actions to purity and chastity. Help me, Lord, never to give up the fight and to be able to declare—for the glory of God—that I am free from any attachment to these sins. I ask this in the name of the Father, and of the Son, and of the Holy Spirit. Amen.

Thank you for committing to undertake this journey. The road ahead may seem difficult; the task of traveling it may appear daunting, even impossible.

That is why it is so important to stay focused on the task for today. Committing to chastity for a lifetime may seem like an unachievable goal, but committing to it for today is something that you can accomplish. A wise friend once told me that "living in the future is living in a graceless moment." This is because God is present, as is his grace, here and now in this very moment. Thinking about tomorrow only brings anxiety and worry. As the great Saint Teresa of Calcutta said, "Yesterday is gone, tomorrow has not yet come. We have only today. Let us begin."[18]

Reflection Questions

1. Do you believe you need personal healing from Jesus Christ to experience freedom from sexual addictions?
2. What is a lie you have told yourself that has negatively affected your life?
3. How is your personal relationship with Jesus currently?
4. How can you work to grow closer in this relationship?
5. Where do you need greater healing in your own life? How can you ask for and seek this healing more boldly?

CHAPTER 5

Overcoming the Addiction: The First Steps for Healing (Steps 1–3)

Whether you are the one struggling with these habits or you know someone who is, I am here to tell you there is so much hope and redemption awaiting you or your loved ones. I often work with women who truly desire freedom from these habits, however, due to lack of success in past attempts to remove the addiction, they have become frustrated and typically despair of ever being able to win this battle. I know once I became convinced of my need to overcome these habits, it took years before seeing a substantial transformation.

Only after understanding the emotional, physical, and spiritual harms of pornography and masturbation, recognizing an attachment or potential addiction in your own life, and finally having the conviction to remove it, can you begin the process of receiving freedom. Through coaching women to freedom over the past several years, I have identified six key steps on their journey to root out these habits. Although I call them steps, we as women can be great at multitasking, so know that they can be done out of order, simultaneously, or even several times. What is important is that you have personally reflected on and addressed each of them according to your own needs and experience.

Step 1: Invite Jesus In

No matter where you are currently in your faith life, the most essential aspect to receiving and experiencing interior freedom from these addictions is inviting in the One who loves you beyond reason. When coaching a woman to freedom, I always start by asking her how her relationship with Jesus is.

How often do you talk to him?

What do your conversations entail?

Have you ever talked to him about your sexual additions? If so, what does he say?

Many times, these are very difficult questions to answer at first. Even if a woman has a deep prayer life, the chances that she has openly brought this into her prayer are small, and if she has, it is often with immense guilt and shame, which keeps the Lord from actually being heard. The sensitivity and cultural stigma wrapped around these issues for women (especially Christian women) have created two common barriers to truly inviting Jesus into their struggle:

1. Shame and fear that the Lord can't love or forgive them amid this "unthinkable" struggle
2. Anger and frustration that the Lord has yet to remove this addiction from their lives

Both of these barriers seem to forget the vast love, power, and mercy of Our Lord. Let's break down where each of these thoughts comes from to know how to root them out:

The first comes from the lie that there is an unforgivable sin, or that the person sinning is, in herself, unworthy of being forgiven. If anyone came to you and said these words, you would, of course, say they were crazy; but as we saw from my experience in the last chapter, these thoughts can be deafening in our minds if we are wrestling with the shame of sexual addiction. I recommend going back to Scripture to be reminded that there is no sin too great for Jesus Christ. The story of the women at the well (John 4:4–42) is a great place to start.

Here, we see Jesus (a Jewish man) approaching a Samaritan woman drawing water from the well in the middle of the day. She is all alone and is startled when Jesus begins talking with her. From the context of the story, we know she is an outcast, otherwise she wouldn't be alone retrieving water during the heat of the day. Jewish people often didn't associate with Samaritans, let alone a man addressing a woman who is considered an outcast by society. And yet Jesus approaches her. In their conversation, Jesus reveals he knows of her past, that she has had multiple husbands, and yet he still calls upon her with an invitation to himself and offers her living water. In Scripture, Jesus rarely verbally reveals his Divine nature to others, but chooses to do so to the woman in this interaction. Though she is a "sinner," Jesus reveals himself to her and invites her to be fully honest in revealing herself to him as well.

That's what Jesus truly desires—unity with you. The lie that your sin is too big for him or that you are unworthy of his forgiveness is what is keeping him from telling you that you are worth everything in the entire universe. He is revealing himself to you constantly, and all you need to do is receive his love and mercy. He is brokenhearted that our culture has brought this addiction upon you, and all he desires is for you to remain in him. Invite him into this struggle by letting him love you through it, not despite it.

The second barrier comes from the belief that this sin defines you, and your lack of trust in God's goodness. The lie is: if your sexual addiction defines your holiness and you are still struggling to overcome it, you must be a terrible Christian. After trying multiple things to get rid of my addiction, the evil one had me believing I must not love Jesus enough, or that something was wrong with me if he couldn't heal me even though I was asking him to. The truth goes back to what we have been saying all along—that sexual sin such as pornography or masturbation are mere symptoms, not the root issue of what is truly going on. Many times, there is much more that God wants to do to transform our hearts, things that go beyond sexual sin, and that takes time.

While I have worked with a few women whom Jesus has healed quickly or even immediately from this habit, if you keep struggling with it, it may be because Jesus wants to heal more in you than only this. As my journey to full freedom took many years, it was during that time when I grew in greater personal humility, compassion for others and their struggles, a better understanding of my brokenness, and the ability to more fully receive the love of the Father. If Jesus had simply removed my temptations or struggles in the beginning like I wanted him to, I would never have learned how to rely more fully on him and be embraced in his mercy. These graces go beyond any desire for a quick fix. Therefore, if you are frustrated with Jesus because you still have this struggle after many attempts to be free, start to ask him how you can better rely on him to overcome it, or ask what more he desires for you to discover about yourself that needs greater transformation or healing. Jesus wants to heal all of us, not just our sexual impurity.

Step 2: Evaluate Your Experience

As difficult as it may be, it is essential for you to personally reflect on and evaluate your own experience with these habits. Going back to your first exposure and walking through the various events that led you to where you are today can be very helpful in recognizing certain patterns of behavior or potential triggers of temptation. It is also helpful for you to recall where Jesus was in these moments or experiences. You need to learn through your reflection that this was not your fault. This is something that happened to you because of the brokenness in our world, the culture, or an individual. You were an innocent victim, and Jesus' heart was broken to watch as this happened to you.

Below are a few questions that can help begin your personal evaluation. Rather than rushing through the list, consider them slowly:

- When were you first exposed to pornography or masturbation?

- How old were you?
- Do you remember what happened?
- Were there other people present who introduced you?
- You should eventually walk through the process of forgiving anyone who may have contributed to your addiction.
- Was there abuse or any additional factors that went into your initial exposure?
- Where was Jesus during this first exposure?
- What was his desire for you in this moment? (Note: He did not desire this for you and is devastated that this happened to you.)
- How did your addiction progress?
- When did the behavior become consistent?
- Are there any key moments when you noticed your addiction increasing in frequency or intensity (the same pattern of behavior wasn't fulfilling anymore, so you moved into something new or more often, etc.)?
- What was going on in your life during these moments of change in behavior?
- Any moments of transition (moving, going to next grade level, etc.) or change in family dynamics (death or birth in the family, divorce, or estranged relationships, etc.)? New romantic relationships or breakups?
- Where was Jesus during all these difficult moments?
- What was his desire for you in these moments?

- Where is your current addiction?
- What is your frequency of watching pornography or masturbating?
- Where do you seek pornography (websites, books, magazines, movies, etc.)?
- What kind do you gravitate toward? What scenarios and/or types do you find yourself seeking?
- Do you use any devices or sex toys?
- Do you desire full freedom from these habits?

You can answer the above for personal reflection, but you don't need to evaluate your experience by yourself. Often it's helpful to have a trained spiritual director or professional Catholic counselor walk you through these questions and experiences to make sure you are reflecting on them appropriately. Until you've been able to correctly identify when and how the addiction began, it can be difficult to root out the causes that went into it.

For me, it was important to recognize my addiction started as an accident, from youthful curiosity. Then, due to typical teenage stress factors as well as some strained family relationships, I unconsciously used masturbation to give me the feeling of love and comfort that I was seeking in other areas of my life. Whether it was a difficult test, a breakup, or a search for more meaning in my life, my sexual addiction was something I could always fall back on for momentary relief. Jesus wept every time I turned to this artificial and harmful version of a lesser "love" as he was waiting with open arms for me to come to him. He was the answer I was always looking for, but I was looking in the other direction. By learning this from reflecting on my previous experiences, I was better prepared for future temptations and experiences that may be triggers for my addiction.

Step 3: Identify Triggers

After evaluating your past experiences, try to pull out potential triggers that may be influencing your current addiction. For this step, the past six months to a year can be the most effective time period to see how your addiction currently is affecting you the most. Common triggers for pornography and masturbation for women include loneliness, stress, exhaustion, insecurities, and hormonal cycle. When trying to identify your triggers, remember that both internal and external factors lead to stronger temptation. Let's examine those next:

Internal triggers are the factors that are in play within you, such as emotional or hormonal conditions that may be increasing your temptation without you being fully aware. Examples of internal triggers include increased stress due to an upcoming test or class project, increased exhaustion from lack of sleep, feeling lonely due to a recent breakup or lack of a relationship, transition in life, or hormonal changes during your monthly time of ovulation.

External triggers are the situational factors that may also be increasing temptation. These involve your specific sexual habits, including the time of day you typically watch pornography or masturbate, location where you do these things (in your bed, shower, etc.), or what type of media you go to for pornography. External triggers could be things like being at home alone, having your phone in your bed at night, not having weekend plans, or going home for holiday breaks.

Know Your Cycle

I need to specifically address your hormonal cycle, which is unique to a woman's experience with these sexual addictions. As you begin to root out sexual addictions from daily or weekly habits, many times women will struggle to overcome the "once-a-month hurdle." Essentially, you may begin to feel freedom from these addictions for weeks, until all of a sudden, bam! It's all you can think about. You'll wake up one morning with it on your mind, maybe notice you are more physically attracted to people who you weren't attracted to before, or crave watching a marathon of chick flicks.

Most often women will tell me they have been steadily working toward freedom in their sexual addiction, but they can't seem to break this once-a-month habit. They will describe an overwhelming surge of thoughts or desires that simply weren't there the day before. This is because your body is producing hormones during a time of ovulation that is directly telling your body to be more intimate with another (as your body is preparing itself for the potential of creating life).

While all women's cycles look different, a basic timeline for the average cycle goes something like this: If you started from day 1 of your period, you will typically bleed for roughly 4–7 days, have 7 or more days "off," and then your body will release an egg during ovulation (while ovulation only happens on one day per cycle, there are 4–7 days surrounding ovulation when your body is considered fertile). This is followed by another week or so "off" until you finally start with your period all over again.

While it's obvious to know when you're on your period (hello Aunt Sally), knowing exactly when you ovulate can be more difficult. An oversimplified way to track your ovulation in order to overcome sexual addictions is this: begin to note times of heavy vaginal mucus while wiping in the bathroom. Many women don't realize this large amount of clear or white discharge is a sign that your body is releasing an egg, and consequently releasing a surge of chemicals that increase your drive for sexual intimacy along with it. You will notice heavy mucus and the surge of hormones during those 4–7 days of fertility on average. After tracking this time of ovulation and fertility within your cycle for a few months, you hopefully will notice a pattern of timing and can begin putting your times of ovulation on the calendar to better prepare for these periods of increased temptation. If this is a heavy trigger for you and you have trouble tracking your specific ovulation time each month, I recommend taking classes from a trained Natural Family Planning instructor who can help walk you through your cycle. You can also download NFP apps that will help you track your cycle (see recommendations in the appendix).

While ovulation may increase our temptation to sexual sin, our hormonal cycles are a beautiful gift we have as women, and we therefore shouldn't be frustrated with our bodies. Instead, we have the opportunity to track our cycles to know when we are ovulating each month and then to find healthier outlets and alternatives to our sexual desires. These can include being more emotionally intimate with Christ or other friends and family in our life during this period of time. This is a beautiful time to grow in our friendships or learn greater detachment for ourselves to be even freer in our lives.

Reflection Questions

1. What does your prayer life currently look like?
2. Have you invited Jesus into your struggle with sexual purity? If not, how can you begin to do so?
3. When evaluating your experience with pornography or masturbation, did you discover anything that surprised you?
4. What do you think are the main triggers that hinder you from achieving freedom from these addictions?
5. Do you currently track your hormonal cycle to know when times of ovulation are? If more people knew of this incredible gift and powerful understanding, how do you think the culture would change?

CHAPTER 6

Overcoming the Addiction: The Disciplines to Implement (Steps 4–6)

Step 4: Create a Plan

Once you've appropriately identified your main triggers, it's time to create a plan and remove or address as many of them as possible. You may go through this process several times as you learn new triggers you didn't initially recognize. To create a good plan for yourself moving forward, try to see these triggers as things you not only need to remove from your daily and weekly habits, but as an opportunity to add potential things to your daily and weekly habits to stay on track.

Let's create a plan using an example from a woman I have worked with—let's call her Katie. In steps 1 through 3, Katie has identified the following:

- She typically watches pornography at night in bed when she doesn't have other plans or homework.
- She has a few websites she goes to on her computer or phone, but also has a few romantic novels she enjoys.
- Temptation heavily increases with stress from schoolwork and tests.
- Temptation is also higher on weekends, and especially if her housemates are out of town or if she is ovulating.
- She has used devices in the past for masturbation, but not every time.
- She was exposed to pornography at a high school party, and it became a daily habit in college.
- She has yet to talk to Jesus about her addiction, and although she attends Mass every Sunday, she doesn't have a consistent prayer life.

From the things she has listed, there are a few clear actions Katie should take:

First, she needs to throw away all materials or devices used primarily for her sexual addictions. All romantic novels, magazines, movies, and devices used for masturbation need to be discarded immediately. I have coached women who have had to throw out ordinary books, magazines, and movies, change lotions (if the scent triggered greater temptation), degrade to a "dumb phone," and even one who donated her iPad.

If there is not an absolute need to own something, there is no reason to add to your temptation as you are striving for uncompromising freedom.

Next, Katie should plan out her semester schedule in advance. With all of her class syllabuses and tentative schedules of her housemates' travel plans over the semester, she should look ahead to see when times of greater temptation will occur. As plans can change, it will be important for her to update it frequently. During test weeks, time when housemates are away, or weeks of ovulation, she should make plans including getting more sleep during test weeks, creating study-date opportunities ahead of time with classmates or friends, inviting friends to stay over on certain weekends, making her own travel plans, etc. Any time when her ovulation week overlaps with these times should get extra attention.

Looking at her pattern of behavior, it seems that loneliness is the main trigger for Katie, so adding positive habits to her routine to address this would be helpful. Habits such as calling three friends a week, setting a friend lunch date every weekend, or decreasing daily time on social media (which leads to an increase in loneliness) could be very effective. If and when a moment of temptation comes to mind, Katie should have a plan ready—going for a walk, calling a friend, or at minimum, getting up from bed to get a drink of water, etc. Katie should also invest in an alarm clock to be able to keep her phone and computer outside her bedroom at night.

Finally, she should create a spirituality plan that includes goals of daily prayer and going to confession regularly. Establishing a habit of twenty to thirty minutes of daily personal prayer will help positively reinforce Katie's desire to feel loved unconditionally as her relationship with Jesus Christ grows. Remember: part of the cause of these addictions is the loss of our identity in the love we were made for; therefore, we are only going to break free from it if we take time each day to be reminded of the love we truly deserve. The same goes for the sacrament of confession. To make sure that this addiction does not define her or her spiritual life, Katie should go to confession regularly to continually reunite herself with Jesus as she seeks freedom—without hiding any sins from her confessor.

An organization designed to help people seek freedom from sexual addictions, Integrity Restored, introduced me to an easy method to put this all in one place, called the freedom plan. See an example of the freedom plan below, where the center section is the habit(s) the person is trying to root out, the middle section contains the negative triggers they want to remove, and the outer layer includes the positive things they plan to add to their life. This freedom plan can be created by anyone for any type of bad habit or addiction they are trying to remove from their life.

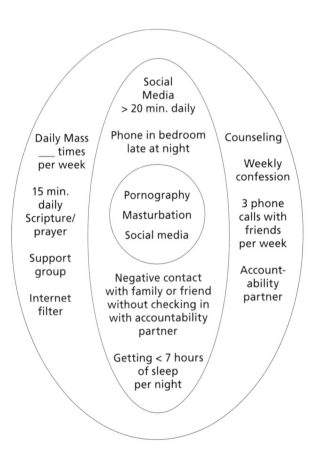

Social
Media
> 20 min. daily

Daily Mass
___ times
per week

Phone in bedroom
late at night

Counseling

Weekly
confession

15 min.
daily
Scripture/
prayer

Pornography

Masturbation

Social media

3 phone
calls with
friends
per week

Support
group

Account-
ability
partner

Internet
filter

Negative contact
with family or friend
without checking in
with accountability
partner

Getting < 7 hours
of sleep
per night

Step 5: Establish Accountability

As you create your plan, you should be working with an accountability partner to help monitor yourself and the plan's effectiveness to make sure you are taking the steps needed to achieve freedom. This person should preferably be close to you and someone you feel comfortable talking with about these sensitive topics. While I highly encourage spiritual direction and/or counseling (see step 6), it is equally important for you to have an accountability partner.

Depending on the frequency of your habit, you should reach out to them daily or weekly as well as during every moment of trigger or temptation. This doesn't mean after you fall, but every time a trigger hits (e.g., if you see an arousing movie scene, have a stressful conversation with someone, or maybe just feel lonely one evening, you should reach out to your accountability partner). This way, you are seeking help before you fall, your accountability partner can be praying for you, and you also are putting into practice good self-awareness, which will allow you to recognize other areas of your life that may need stronger discipline.

Finally, your accountability partner should be someone of the same gender. If you are married, although your spouse can be aware of your freedom plan, it is important to have someone you are not romantically involved with to support and encourage you on your path to freedom as well.

In addition to the removal of devices and changes in patterns of behavior your plan will be monitoring, also discuss with your accountability partner other potential means that will help in your healing—e.g., Do you need an internet block, such as Covenant Eyes or Qustodio? Do you need to seek professional counseling? Should you attend a healing retreat or a sexual addiction program? Some of these questions can better be answered by a spiritual director or counselor. However, your accountability partner can offer helpful encouragement as well as be a motivator to make sure you follow through on these things. Other resources available for women can be found in the appendix.

Step 6: Seek Spiritual Healing and Professional Counseling

As you begin to take significant steps in your journey toward sexual freedom and healing, there may be times when you succumb to temptation. In these times, you must embrace God's mercy and seek his forgiveness through the sacrament of confession. As Catholics, we confess our sins to God through a priest and ask for God's forgiveness and reconciliation with Christ and his Church. This sacrament can be intimidating, especially in the midst of sexual sin, yet it is extremely grace-filled and beautiful. Furthermore, the more often you go, the better at facing temptation you will become.

When I was overcoming my addiction, it was the continual healing received through confession that allowed me to go longer each time between falls. I also established certain parameters for myself to aid in moments of temptation. For example, I started going to confession face-to-face with the priest and made sure to use the word "masturbation" in my confession rather than saying "personal impurity" or some other phrase that made me "feel" more off the hook. I required myself not to commit additional sin by receiving the Eucharist at Mass if I had fallen and not been to confession (since any severe sin such as masturbation requires you to be cleansed in confession before receiving his Divinity in the Eucharist). Finally, I forced myself to go to a priest I knew personally each time I fell so I couldn't hide behind the false idea that a different priest meant I had less sin to admit to. In the end, Jesus is the same Jesus in every confession, so while these parameters didn't and don't change the forgiveness received in confession, they were added incentive to keep me from falling into temptation when it came.

I would also recommend going to confession more often than you typically fall into the sin of sexual impurity. Meaning, if you fall every few months, you should go to confession monthly; if you fall every month, weekly; and if you fall weekly; go to confession multiple times in a week. The purpose of this is not to make you overly scrupulous or become overwhelmed by your sins, but rather to remind you that the sin of pornography or masturbation does not define you. There is so much more healing and encouragement Jesus wants to do in your heart, and often we are so blinded by our sexual sin that we rarely give God a chance to transform us in other ways. Getting into the practice of admitting to other struggles in your life and allowing Jesus to work on those can be profoundly healing and can help you to stop seeing your sexual impurity as your identity.

Lastly, depending on your experience, having a professional help you work through any past wounds or deeper causes of this addiction may be the final part of fully removing this habit from your life. While it can be a final step, I often recommend counseling and/or spiritual direction immediately for women who want freedom from pornography and masturbation. If your desire to engage in these sexual behaviors comes from a deeper wound or an effort to avoid or to numb other emotions or experiences you are going through, these are things only a trained professional can help you explore. Without going deeper, you may never be able to completely root out the temptation, because it's the only thing you have convinced yourself will "keep you safe" from whatever else happened or is currently happening in your life.

When seeking a good counselor, make sure to read through their background and specialties to make sure they have experience with what you may be bringing into a session. I have worked with women who have been to counselors who promote pornography and masturbation as acceptable and even "healthy behaviors," which is counterproductive, so confirm that your counselor has the same understanding of the harms of these sexual addictions. If possible, having a Catholic or Christian counselor who is trained to use prayer and other spiritual components will only better reinforce all the steps we've addressed to seeking full freedom and healing.

Starting Over

For many young women who have not yet pursued total freedom, the question of falling into sin is not a matter of if but when. Habits of sin—vices—are not easily unlearned. It can be demoralizing and difficult when you fall. You may get down on yourself and feel like giving up the fight.

I have three words to say to that:

Don't give up!

Every fall should be a learning experience. It allows you to identify the wound in your life and to pray within the pain of that wound. It presents an opportunity for you to experience God's love and mercy in the sacrament of confession. It helps you to identify your vulnerabilities so that you learn to guard yourself better next time. It helps to strengthen you so that you are fiercer when temptation strikes again. Victory is possible. When you fall, don't lose heart: in wars, the winning side has usually lost some of the battles along the road to victory.

For me, the war was won by fighting one battle at a time. Amid temptation, being fully free for the rest of my life seemed impossible. Yet when I decided to take each temptation as it came, I said to myself, "I am going to beat this one temptation." This gave me confidence, and I began winning more battles than I lost. As a result, I gained even more confidence. I won more and more battles until, one day, I found I no longer was enslaved to habits of impurity. It wasn't that temptations never came again; it's that I knew I could beat any temptation because I had done so before.

Reflection Questions

1. Based on your triggers, what are the ways you can best monitor yourself to avoid future circumstances of temptation?

2. What do you think of creating a personal freedom plan? What are some things you would put on yours?

3. Who is someone you could talk to about your struggles as a good accountability partner?
4. How regularly do you receive the sacrament of confession? What goals do you have now for receiving this sacrament more often?
5. What other ways could be beneficial to you in your journey to experiencing true freedom (e.g., spiritual direction, professional counseling, retreats, support groups, etc.)?

CHAPTER 7

Help! I'm in a Relationship with a Porn Addict

By Everett Fritz

No matter where you stand in your journey to uncompromising purity, an equally important aspect to address with pornography and masturbation is how to properly navigate a relationship in which your partner may have a history with these things as well.

I am involved in several marriage forums on social media. Daily, it seems that wives lament their feelings of despair and helplessness in dealing with their husband's pornography addiction.

Stories run the gamut of all kinds of life-crippling behaviors. I've heard of husbands being fired for repeatedly getting caught looking at pornography at work. I heard a story of a husband who repeatedly was caught with prostitutes because he was seeking to act out his pornography fantasies. It is common to hear of couples dealing with the husband's erectile dysfunction because of repeated use of masturbation and pornography.

In my role in ministry, I have been in situations where I have helped dating and married men who suffer from pornography addiction. The number one thing I hear is the complaint that their significant other "rips into them" daily because of their addiction. The woman is suffering as a result of her partner's lack of fidelity, and the woman emotionally regulates her pain by verbally tearing her partner apart. While the verbal bashing is understandable, it feeds into the man's shame and feelings of inadequacy, which pushes him back to porn as a means to escape his suffering.

This kind of relationship between a man and a woman is toxic and both end up suffering. If you are in a position where you are dating, engaged to, or married to a man with a pornography addiction, you are not alone. This is an epidemic problem. The journey to freedom is difficult and many factors may be beyond your control. The good news is that there is hope and relationships can be transformed.

What Can You Do?

The advice I give below should be taken as encouragement for increasing your discernment. If you are not praying regularly, this should be the first red flag that something is off. God has an amazing plan for your life and your partner's life. Unfortunately, you cannot know that plan unless you are consistently seeking a relationship with Jesus. Your relationship with Jesus needs to be consistent because he seldom lays out all the details of his plan at once. There is a wisdom to this. If Jesus told Saint Peter when they first met that his path to heaven would include martyrdom, Peter likely would not have followed Jesus and we would not have had Peter's leadership and gifts in the early Church.

Accompanying someone with pornography addiction (especially if that someone is a boyfriend or spouse) is not easy and can be a painful journey. Daily prayer and seeking Christ's will has to be a prerequisite to any attempt to help someone with this addiction.

With that in mind, there are three categories I believe relationships fall into regarding this subject. My advice is different depending on which category your relationship falls under.

Category 1: Your boyfriend doesn't see a problem with his pornography addiction.

If you are dating a guy who looks at pornography and doesn't believe it is a big deal, the only thing that you can do to help him is to break up with him.

A dating relationship will always end in one of two ways: marriage or breakup. Few couples date for thirty years. If you know that the person you are dating is not the one you want to marry, then you should end the relationship. The conclusion is inevitable, and delaying it for any reason can set the stage for even more pain and suffering long term.

Pornography inhibits a person's capacity to love. It conditions a person to use others as objects for selfish gratification rather than to cherish a person who is made in the image and likeness of God. It is one thing to be struggling with sin because of an attachment to the sin. It is another thing entirely to justify your sin and fail to acknowledge the damage that it causes.

Missionary dating (dating for the sake of trying to help someone or "save their soul") seldom works out. While the man you are dating may one day recognize the damage that pornography is doing to your life and his, you needn't waste your time waiting for him to awaken to the need to develop virtue. Breaking up with him may be the most loving thing you can do, because it sends the message that his pornography addiction isn't acceptable and is the reason why you are walking out of his life.

Don't wait. End the relationship immediately.

Category 2: Your boyfriend, fiancé, or husband is seeking help for his pornography addiction.
Discerning the future of your relationship is not as black and white if your man falls into this category. While breaking off the relationship would be acceptable for all the reasons listed in the previous category, there may be justifiable reasons to remain in the relationship if he truly is seeking freedom from his addiction and is making progress. It is also important that he is personally motivated to break free and is not simply "trying" to stop the habit because it bothers you. Viewing pornography is an act of infidelity and needs to be recognized as such. This isn't just "something all guys do." It's something all true men renounce!

With that having been said, it is helpful to remember that many men develop attachments to porn long before they become men. Many of the men who have addictions to pornography were first exposed when they were children. I have had teenagers in my youth ministry tell me that they first discovered porn when they were six years old.

I encountered pornography for the first time when I discovered my uncle's stack of *Playboy* magazines in a closet. While I could have looked away from the magazines, my sense of virtue was not well developed enough and my curiosity was that of a child.

Although a man is responsible for the choices he makes and bears the responsibility to break the addiction, you may find you have more compassion for his ailment if you understand he may have fallen into this addiction at a very young age. But because he is no longer a child, he must take responsibility for his choices.

If you choose to remain in a relationship with a guy who is addicted to pornography, there need to be expectations that he is doing everything in his power to overcome the addiction. At a minimum, he should have accountability in his life—someone other than you who holds him responsible for his actions. He should have filters on all of his devices (like Covenant Eyes or Qustodio), and he should be involved in support groups or regular mentoring. It would also be advisable that he seek counseling or at least regular spiritual direction.

In addition to praying for him (and giving him a copy of my book, *Freedom*), you need to be kept apprised of his progress in developing virtue. If you are not married, I recommend laying out expectations concerning what you want to see before you move forward in your relationship.

Category 3: You are married to a man who looks at pornography and he isn't interested in change.

This is the most difficult situation if you are in a relationship with someone who has a pornography addiction. I can't begin to understand the pain and feelings of rejection and inadequacy that go along with this. Thankfully, matrimony is a sacrament and because of its sacramental nature, there is grace that is available to you. Start by praying for an outpouring of the graces of the sacrament in your marriage.

While your husband may not be willing to seek help for his addiction, this shouldn't prevent you from seeking help. Go to a counselor, a respected pastor, or even friends to find a community of support. While your husband may not be willing to join you in marriage counseling, you can start by attending marriage counseling on your own. Marriage counselors may have suggestions on ways in which you can positively encourage your husband to seek the help he needs.

Finally, if your husband is physically or emotionally abusive (and pornography addiction tends to develop these behaviors in a man), then I recommend separating immediately. If children are involved in your relationship, this may be difficult to do. However, separation is what you need to heal and the only way to remove yourself from an abusive relationship. Separation does not mean that you have to get divorced, but it does send the message that you will not accept or tolerate his abuse.

Kelsey's Perspective

Ladies, my heart is broken by what pornography and masturbation have done to our world, specifically, to the men in our lives. Although we may have been fighting this fight alongside them, no one can deny how intensely men have been targeted for generations. When I encounter women who carry the heavy burden of being in a relationship with someone with a pornography addiction, there are two common lies I hear:

"Men need pornography and masturbation, especially if they aren't 'getting it' from me."

Often, women are fed and believe the lie that men are "uncontrollable animals" with greater biological/sexual urges than women, and therefore it is not only natural but necessary for men to seek and receive sexual pleasure once they reach puberty. "If we aren't having sex, they need to get a release somehow!" or "Even if we do have sex, him exploring other avenues is completely natural."

While men's sexual desires do increase as their hormones change (as do women's, might I add), this does not justify needing to act on these impulses or not learning how to order them properly to live out of total freedom. The alternative is being a slave to our impulses, which is harmful to ourselves and society as a whole. As humans, we have a significant amount of self-control and choice in our actions (different from animals), which can be seen in our ability to eat healthy food (rather than chocolate cake for every meal), to choose to exercise, or even to deny ourselves basic needs, like fasting from food for spiritual reasons. The Church teaches that choosing these goods will help us build stamina and the virtue necessary to be able to combat other temptations, such as lust of the flesh.

Furthermore, I know several men and women who have never had sex who are beyond happy with their lives. If it was truly necessary, how is this possible? How come all the men and women who have not engaged in masturbation, fornication, or premarital sex haven't spontaneously combusted or gone mad? While living in sexual freedom can take great effort, especially with initial exposure to something like pornography or masturbation, it is very possible. The goal is not simply to repress our sexual urges, but rather to allow our sexual desires to be transformed through recognizing that authentic love should always will the good of the other. Men and women who live in sexual freedom are free to engage in relationships without the enslavement of lust or divided interest of the heart. Therefore, setting the standard in your relationship that someone must live in sexual freedom or be actively working toward it to pursue you romantically should be nonnegotiable.

"It will stop once we are married."

As mentioned earlier, sexual sins and behavior are deeply rooted and can be heavily entangled in our brain chemistry, depending on the extent and length of the addiction. While the lie "the addiction will stop once we are married" is based on the hope of human transformation that is possible through Christ, this transformation can only be possible if the person recognizes the need to change their behavior immediately. Your boyfriend should understand the need to seek freedom in Christ and to seek healing rather than wait until there is a lifelong commitment made. Marriage is not a cure-all for ailments or addictions. On the contrary, when it comes to sexual sins of our past, these things often come swinging into marriage like a wrecking ball, and unless both people have taken the time and steps necessary to pursue sexual freedom, marriage will be incredibly difficult and potentially harmful for both of you. If your significant other struggles with these things currently, I encourage you to delay taking the next step in your relationship (whether that means waiting to get engaged or moving your wedding date back) in order for the necessary healing to take place.

In light of both of these lies, I want to remind you that you are not your boyfriend's savior. He already has one, and his name is Jesus Christ. Staying with someone in hopes they change their mind or will become a better person because of you (or as Everett called it, missionary dating) seldom works out because it's not truly loving the other, it's selfishly loving the feeling of being a "hero" and loving who someone could be without giving them the best opportunity to become that person. Ending a relationship or delaying the next step forward is an act of love to give them the time for healing, as well as communicating the proper expectations for your relationship. During this time, he can seek out stronger male friendships, engage in deeper spiritual direction, prayer, and accountability, and hopefully become the man Christ has called him to be. If God has called this man to be your future spouse, we must pray and trust that God will do the heavy lifting and it will be made possible in his timing, not ours. This surrendering of your relationship and ultimately your vocation to Christ will only improve your future marriage, and I promise you will never regret it.

If you are already married, I agree and further emphasize Everett's point of seeking outside help, whether through professional counseling or spiritual direction. Allow others to speak truth into your situation and realize you do not have to endure this suffering alone. There are communities of support as well as Christ's love and mercy to enter more deeply into, as this experience doesn't have to define your life or your marriage forever.

When to Bring It Up

If you are beginning a new romantic relationship, or plan to in the future, many of you may be wondering how to bring up this important topic with your partner. While there is no perfect recipe for success, the entire conversation should be done with prudence and sensitivity. It's important to allow a relationship to develop naturally and not force conversations too soon or divulge too much of your heart early on. Because of this, I recommend being discreet in the beginning, whether it's in asking questions or sharing your own experience.

A good opportunity to mention it casually is when you are having a conversation about becoming "exclusive." As you and your significant other discern to move forward into intentional dating, conversations on personal boundaries and chastity should come up. During this conversation, mention that you are aware of how much pornography and masturbation are currently affecting our world. Ask him if he has proper accountability and support in these areas as it is your desire and expectation in your relationship that you both are pursuing sexual freedom. If you have accountability in these areas, feel free to share with him that you are personally pursuing freedom and have accountability as well.

Notice, there is no need to get more specific or ask for more details at this stage in the relationship. This is simply to establish expectations, and if he doesn't have accountability in these areas or acknowledge a need to change, this brief mention provides an opportunity to invite him to seek counsel from other men and spiritual mentors before moving forward in the relationship.

While it may seem abrupt or intimidating to bring up this topic, checking in and making sure you both have outside accountability in all areas of chastity will only make your relationship stronger and more successful. With the guidance of a spiritual director or mentor as the relationship develops closer to engagement or marriage, you both can begin sharing more of your experience to navigate through these sensitive areas as they apply to your situations.

Reflection Questions

1. How have you seen pornography affect the culture of men in today's society?
2. Have you personally navigated a conversation with a significant other regarding their experience with pornography or masturbation? How did it go?
3. How could ending a relationship (even when

you love someone) truly be an act of love if pornography or masturbation is something they struggle with?

4. How can we as women help encourage and support men in our lives to pursue sexual freedom?

5. Which of the lies Kelsey mentioned, or others, have you believed when it comes to a man's viewing of pornography?

CHAPTER 8

I've Been Abused

Alongside pornography and masturbation, there are other factors that are part of this conversation. From my work in this ministry, it is important to address a few of them, especially if any of these are part of your personal experience. While I might not be able to touch on every possible situation you have questions about, I hope to provide enough insight to lead you in the right direction.

Physical Abuse

If you or anyone you know has a history or an experience of being physically abused in any way, I highly recommend seeking professional counseling and taking this deeply with you into prayer. Abuse of every kind distorts our view of the world, relationships, and ourselves in a way many of us can't explain. Often, these events of abuse can be the catalyst to sexual addiction and a difficult trigger to combat if ongoing.

Physical abuse is when someone has used their power over you in an attempt to threaten, punish, or establish dominance. Through doing so, they may have convinced you that you are "nothing," or that you might even deserve this treatment. There is no love in this act, and certainly no room for excuses on their behalf. The use of drugs, alcohol, or other substances are not avenues that make physical abuse excusable, nor is the promise that it won't happen again.

Someone willing to hit, shove, or tower over you in an attempt to physically scare you are tactics used by someone whose experience in the world has been shaped and distorted by violence, and it is unlikely that this is the only or last time it will happen. Whether it's through their past experiences, extensive viewing of violence in media or pornography, or personal anger that has built up over time, you are not capable of handling their problems by yourself. If you are in a family relationship, a romantic relationship, or marriage, this person needs to seek professional help before you can even consider the possibility of maintaining a healthy, loving relationship with them. Supporting and encouraging them to seek help while also maintaining your distance so they can receive this help is crucial. Depending on the extent of the relationship, you should immediately sever all ties either permanently or until an extensive period of time and healing has been made possible for both of you. Your first priority needs to be your safety, not salvaging the relationship.

Finally, telling someone or the authorities to assist you out of your situation, even if it may get that person temporarily in trouble, is truly loving them. No person should have to carry around that type of anger or rage, as all of us are made in the image and beauty of our Creator. By bringing this truth to the light, you are aiding them on the path to true freedom. You are not alone in your fight and shouldn't have to compromise your life out of protection or fear of anyone.

Emotional Abuse

Similar to physical abuse, this type of abuse distorts our understanding of the world and our relationships as well and can lead to various addictions. Unfortunately, emotional abuse often goes undetected much longer. To know if you are currently or have ever been in an emotionally abusive relationship, think critically and honestly about how the people you spend time with most make you feel. After spending time with someone, do you feel better about yourself, or worse? Do you feel encouraged, supported, and uplifted, or do you feel embarrassed, ashamed, and worthless?

Every relationship is different, but certain friendships or romantic relationships can try to manipulate you emotionally by making you feel like you are the one who is always at fault. They will make you feel worthless, or that you aren't truly loving them unless you do X, Y, or Z. In high school, I remember a "friend" once tell me I was "nothing and everyone knew it" because I didn't sit with them at lunch. So, while it might seem small, these comments and types of manipulations can stay with us for a long time.

People who emotionally abuse you don't always seem harmful at the beginning. Particularly with romantic relationships, many times we will put up with little negative comments here and there to feel the love and belonging that comes from being with them. However, these comments can lead to truly damaging images of ourselves. We hope that one day the person will see how amazing we are, and will maybe start treating us better. What happens, however, is we continue to convince ourselves we aren't yet worthy of being loved and will continue to compromise our standards to "finally" get the treatment we deserve.

Emotional abuse can often feed our addictions to pornography and masturbation to receive a more beneficial love without the cost or pain of emotional abuse. If you haven't figured it out, it's time to dump him or change friends if these patterns persist. Losing a relationship, or several, is worth regaining the dignity you were created for. For those in emotionally abusive marriages, I encourage you both to seek professional counseling to root out where the insecurities might be gaining control in your relationship.

Sexual Abuse

This is the most common form of abuse we see that has the greatest impact on women's sexual purity today. If we couldn't tell by *Time*'s 2017 Person of the Year (the #metoo movement "Silence Breakers"), more and more women are coming out with exhaustive stories of sexual abuse and long-term harassment in the workplace and at home. Is this news? Unfortunately not. Approximately one in five women reports completed or attempted rape during their lifetime, with 43.6% of women in the United States claiming some type of forced sexual contact.[19] This includes all types of fornication including groping, the pressure to go further sexually than desired, or full-on sexual assault and rape.

In most cases, these individuals knew their attacker, which makes it that much harder to reveal the truth or gain personal healing. Whether it was a friend, family member, or stranger, you must remember it was not your fault. You never asked for this to happen, nor did you lead them on to assume your no actually meant yes. Through this event or series of sexual abuse, you have potentially lost trust in yourself, forgotten that sex is a life-giving gift from God, and/or believe that establishments of protection will most likely let you down (family, the general public, etc.).

In college, I knew a woman who was very aware of her eccentric sexual behaviors and even considered herself a sexaholic (she was proud of it). One night she confided in me that she thinks she would have remained a virgin until marriage if she hadn't been raped in high school. She was currently having sex with multiple different men each week and she told me, "My power to say yes every time now is for the one time my choice to say no was taken away." This tragically made sense to me. When your sexuality is taken into someone else's control, it's understandable you may desire to seek sexual control in any way you can (through casual sex, pornography, or masturbation).

Extreme avoidance or reacting out of PTSD can also be a common experience after sexual abuse. During my junior year of college, I was going out to my car late at night to pick up some friends. As I was close to my car, I noticed a girl limping across the street and started calling to her as I got closer. To my surprise, she was a freshman from the recruitment group I led earlier that semester. I said her name and she immediately fell into my arms bawling. I picked her up and carried her to my car (her leg was in pretty bad shape). After convincing her to go to the ER,

I discovered the appalling truth of what happened: she had been at a college party earlier that evening, and when a guy she liked in the house invited her to his room to continue "hanging out," she said yes. It still being early in the evening, she thought nothing of it as there were people and loud music everywhere. Once in his room, however, he closed and locked the door behind him. She told him to stop, but by the way he began to aggressively approach her, she quickly looked at her surroundings, opened the window, and jumped . . . from the second floor. As she told me the story, she looked me in the eye and said without flinching, "It might sound crazy, but I was sexually abused many years ago, and there is no way I'm going through that again!"

While it might sound crazy to jump out of a second-story window to avoid a "potential" sexual assault, it doesn't if you've been in a similar situation. Many women experience PTSD after a sexual abuse event and may spend several years running from what happened. This avoidance can turn into several unhealthy actions or addictions and keep you from truly living out of freedom. If this is your experience, it was not your fault, and God did not desire this for you. Recounting your initial exposure to pornography or any damaging sexual experience is crucial to experiencing full freedom. Finally, bringing this to a professional counselor to help begin the healing is key if you desire to root out all other residual sexual habits.

Mutual Masturbation/Oral Sex

"So I can't have sex, watch pornography, or personally masturbate, but if my significant other is the one giving me sexual pleasure that doesn't end in actual intercourse, then surely it's okay?"

Wrong. Mutual masturbation, or the physical stimulation of each other's genitalia outside of the context of ending in vaginal intercourse within marriage is not okay. This includes oral sex, hand stimulation, phone sex, or otherwise. Now, that might seem like a lot of rules, so let me break it down.

We've already established that pornography and masturbation remove the physical intimacy necessary to create a healthy, sexual bond with your future or current spouse. By watching others, or engaging in your sexual-minded fantasies, you are hurting your current or future marriage by not being able to enter into full union. Similarly, we discussed how sex is meant to be not only unitive between you and your spouse, but life-giving. Without this component, the sexual pleasure given and received becomes utilitarian—using another person for personal gratification and use. People can sexually use each other in relationships, even if it's mutually beneficial.

In regard to mutual masturbation, each person is unable to give themselves fully within the sexual pleasure they are giving. Thus, the entire exchange of sexual pleasure becomes a utilitarian transaction where one person gives sexual pleasure only (not to themselves), and the other receives it. This is not unified. While this might be difficult to understand and accept at first, by allowing mutual masturbation to come into your relationship, you will slowly be driving yourselves apart through this mutual use. These acts will also make it more difficult to overcome other sexual addictions.

If this is a current habit for you and your partner, I encourage you to reevaluate the priorities of your relationship and make sure you are on the same page with your desires for sexual purity. If not, break up with him. However, if you are on the same page, create a plan of attack for how you will combat these temptations. For example: don't sit alone with him in a parked car, make sure a roommate is always around when you're with him at home, or maybe cut late-night movies or conversations short, or have a curfew, etc.

Dreams

Throughout my time coaching women in purity, I have had several women approach me with questions regarding their experience of sexual dreams. These dreams generally display a vivid experience for them and can sometimes lead them to wake up mid-orgasm. While this can be alarming when it's happening, and even scarring for the person experiencing it, it's important to note that dreams are not in your control, and therefore you are not culpable (even if the dream leads you to physical orgasm without your consent). However, because it can be very distressing and often causes greater temptation the next day in a woman's battle for purity, it's important to set up a plan for yourself if it happens again (and especially if these dreams are a common occurrence).

Similar to creating a plan for recovery, make sure to have set expectations and a protocol for when you wake up. It is often most helpful to change your environment to not allow the dream to continue into a daydream fantasy. Getting out of bed and getting a drink of water, taking a walk around your house, or even picking up a book to lead you through a guided prayer or meditation can all be helpful ways to clear your mind. If you feel that past abuse or events may be triggering these dreams, it may be helpful to receive counseling to address those deeper issues. With counseling and increased time away from your addiction to pornography, masturbation, or sex, you will most likely see a decreased frequency in these types of dreams.

Violence/S&M

As stated earlier, as an addiction to pornography or masturbation elevates, the viewer will often begin to seek more drastic or aggressive content to receive the same chemical release. In the pornography industry, violent displays or S&M (sadomasochism) content is readily available, and almost always the violence is directed toward women. Due to this, many women often develop a desire for this type of violent sexual relationship in current or future sexual experiences. Men viewing this type of pornography may also encourage this, and with material for women like *Fifty Shades of Grey*, it's no wonder these desires have become a household norm. I have worked with women who are now only sexually excited if there is some form of violence involved in the sexual act. This is unhealthy and will only lead to other unhealthy habits outside and within marriage.

It's obvious when learning about God's true desire for us in our experience of trinitarian love through the sexual experience, that there is no place for violence, force, or threatening aggression in the bedroom. If this is something you notice you are gravitating toward or desire, seek professional and spiritual guidance for healing. Also, be honest with your current or future spouse about lines you may need to draw to not fall into past temptations.

Same-Sex Pornography

Similar to violent content in pornography, some female viewers may also find themselves viewing or even fantasizing about same-sex relations. This does not necessarily mean you have an attraction to the same sex.

Growing up, most of your relationships and friendships with your peers are with members of the same sex. As you reach puberty, your attitude toward the opposite sex typically shifts, and you begin to desire more (and different types of) relationships with them. These opposite-sex relationships are primarily driven by the newly emerging sexual drives tied with physical and psychological growth and your growing desire for love and intimacy. However, puberty isn't like a light switch. Most young women don't go to bed one night and wake up the next morning with sexual desires for the opposite sex. It happens sometimes, as a young woman develops physically and emotionally, that she experiences a vaguely romantic affection for a close friend of the same sex. This feeling is typically fleeting, but can be confusing. It usually ceases as hormone fluctuations ease and the body and mind continue to develop. Women in puberty and even as young adults can experience such an attraction as part of their normal sexual development.

Another important distinction is that some of these desires to view or engage in same-sex relations are what can be called homoemotional-driven desires. This refers to someone with a strong emotional desire to be around members of the same sex. These attractions can come from an unfulfilled male or female relationship in a person's life—like a poor relationship with a mother—that leaves a young woman attracted to the very qualities she feels she does not possess. This emotional attraction can lead to sexual desire and behavior if the wound is not healed, but it is distinctly different from a romantic sexual desire for someone of the same sex.

Unfortunately, in our culture these other potential aspects of same-sex desires are not commonly discussed. This is not to say that all people who identify themselves as homosexual don't truly experience sexual desire for the same sex. Instead, I bring up these examples to show that desires for members of the same sex do not automatically translate to a homosexual orientation. Feelings such as these, especially in teenagers or young adult women, need to be carefully analyzed and reflected upon.

Regardless, if this is the case for you, or if there are deeper, same-sex attractions being felt, you are first and foremost a daughter of our beloved Creator. Our identity always rests in our Father's arms, not our sexual attractions. If you find yourself attracted to same-sex pornography, removing stimulus content and pornography that feeds these desires will help you better live in freedom. Heterosexual and same-sex-attracted women alike are invited and called to live in the same freedom God designed for all of us.

Reflection Questions

1. Are you familiar with any of the topics discussed in this chapter (either personally or from someone you know)? What has been your experience with them?
2. Other than triggering a potential pornography addiction, what are other ways you think emotional abuse affects women today?
3. How have you seen violence increase in today's culture (media/news, movies, TV, video games, etc.)? How do you believe this has shaped our culture?
4. How can we better come alongside our fellow sisters who may be experiencing some of these difficult situations to be one, unified, Body of Christ?

CHAPTER 9

Uncompromising Purity

Over the course of this book, we have covered a lot of information on how to receive freedom from sexual addictions, specifically pornography and masturbation. Hopefully, through everything presented you have come away with a greater conviction of your true identity, as well as some practical ways to begin or continue on your journey to true freedom. Below are a few reminders of the key points we addressed throughout the book. We hope you remember and hold on to each of them as you courageously live out uncompromising purity every day.

Do Not Despair

Whether it was a previous unhealthy relationship that introduced you; physical, emotional, and/or sexual abuse you endured; or unintentional initial exposure to pornography or masturbation at a young age, don't internalize the blame. Jesus did not want this to happen to you, and thinking differently only continues to keep you from the overflowing mercy and love he desires to pour upon you. While there may have been times our decisions or curiosity led us into more difficult situations or heavier addictions, the evil one wants to keep us in personal despair, which is the opposite of freedom. The hard reality is, our culture and world have conditioned us to accept these behaviors and situations as normal, or worse, as beneficial sexual "liberations" that elevate our society's progress from outdated and restrictive practices. This conditioning is why fighting our desire to justify our actions can be so difficult. Keep in mind that your friends, family members, and potential "role models" have also been fed this conditioning, who will continue to challenge any convictions you may have made as you read this book. Recognize that it is not entirely their fault either, but be ready to stand strong in the face of rejection or pushback you may receive from others. This is what being an uncompromising woman is all about.

There Is Hope in Forgiveness

While the initial exposure most likely wasn't your fault, and people in your life may not understand your commitment to uncompromising purity, you have everything in your ability to recognize the changes needed to seek full healing and freedom. In this book, you learned about the magnificent power of the sacrament of confession for your forgiveness, but there is also great power and need to forgive others in your life who may have influenced these addictions as well.

Whenever you are tempted to be angry with people who have hurt you, frustrated over your addiction, or are upset with our oversexualized and exploitative culture, you can pray for forgiveness. Pray for all of the creators of pornography, those in control of the media, those in Hollywood, or any sexual predators who project their brokenness onto others. Through this prayer and forgiveness, countless women have found freedom. While it may seem impossible to achieve, from my personal experience I can tell you that freedom and healing from these addictions do exist, and they exist for you.

God Has a Plan for Your Freedom

You may wonder, "If freedom does exist, and Jesus doesn't want this addiction for me, why am I still struggling?" No matter how much we live from the first two points mentioned, the journey to freedom is unpredictable and often takes more of us than we originally bargained for. As I mentioned earlier, God doesn't want just part of us, so if you think asking for sexual healing and freedom is as simple as asking and receiving, you may be sorely disappointed. While miraculous healing can and does happen, more often than not, God allows us to go on an adventure of self-discovery, wrestling truths of God's love and mercy, learning to view ourselves as his daughter, forgiving people and situations we never knew were burying us, and making small, incremental triumphs by conquering lies and temptations we once believed were in control.

This may seem daunting; however, it is through this process that we begin to truly know the heart of Jesus Christ and trust in his love for us. Therefore, in moments of frustration or doubt, remember to always go back to him. Remember, he has a plan for you and your purity that is far greater than you could ever imagine. His heart breaks every time we fall because he knows we are separating ourselves from him, not because we in ourselves are shameful. Trust his plan for you, trust his love for you, and always remember to entrust your suffering, *your addiction*, to his Sacred Heart.

Living Out This Freedom Will Transform Your Life

Just as there is hope for you to receive freedom, there is hope in the life that awaits you by living out this freedom daily. While our world continues to tell us our power and freedom come from sexual expression and exploitation, women who live out their identity in the

Trinity are more fulfilled and joyful. Consider women who are truly happy and "free": it is the women who have unwavering confidence and strong convictions, distinguished women who know who they are and are unapologetically themselves.

As I began to explore my relationship with Jesus and have moved deeper into a relationship with him, I have never felt more confident in who I am, or rather, *whose* I am. The drama that once encapsulated my friendships or romantic relationships all but disappeared, my outlook on difficult situations or daily sufferings became lighter burdens, and even the typical state of happiness I previously experienced couldn't compare to the deeper peace I have found possible. And while this peace-filled "high" also comes with its share of obstacles, sufferings, and required strength, Jesus is always there to bring us to the next level of encounter with him.

If someone isn't fully convinced that living out purity will transform their life for the better, I ask them to try it for a few months (paired with proper prayer and accountability) to see if they notice a change in themselves or how they experience the world. This includes living boldly as God invites us, not only in sexual freedom but also in other areas we may lack freedom in as well (such as drinking, drugs, social media addictions, etc.). As G.K. Chesterton brilliantly stated, "The Christian ideal has not been tried and found wanting. It has been found difficult; and left untried."[20] To be an uncompromising woman, we need to confront the difficult and courageously give our best. The journey to freedom may not come easy, but it is infinitely worth it.

Let's Stop Compromising

It is time for us to take a stand as women. It's time for us to stop compromising in how we know we deserve to be treated, compromising in how we know others deserve to be loved, and most importantly, compromising in the love we allow to penetrate our hearts and drive our decisions and actions. You are made for so much more than this world offers, and it's time to rightfully live from the true identity you were made for—in the image and likeness of our Creator. We are alongside you on your journey. Know of our prayers and confidence in you, and know that the Holy Spirit to be with you every step of the way.

Reflection Questions

1. Of the reminders mentioned, which one(s) do you think you struggle most believing?
2. Where are other areas you think you lack in freedom (drinking, disordered eating, drugs, technology, social media, shopping, etc.)? How can

you apply the principles learned in this book to some of those other areas?

3. What would the world look like if women lived truly uncompromising lives?

4. Moving forward, what are your personal goals or next steps to living out uncompromising purity?

5. Who else do you think needs to hear or learn about these things? How can you share this truth in journeying toward freedom with them?

Recommended Resources

Programs and Further Coaching

Reclaim Sexual Health Ministries:
   reclaimsexualhealth.com
Fortify Program: joinfortify.com

Ministries

Integrity Restored: integrityrestored.com
Women Made New: womenmadenew.com
Chastity Project: chastity.com
The Porn Effect: theporneffect.com
Fight the New Drug: fighthenewdrug.com

Retreats and Workshops

John Paul II Healing Center: jpiihealingcenter.org
Theology of the Body Institute: tobinstitute.org
Bethesda Workshops: bethesdaworkshops.org

Tools to Overcome Addiction

Covenant Eyes: (for a free month, use promo code: chastity)

Qustodio: qustodio.com

Victory App: thevictoryapp.com

Recovery Tribe: rtribe.org

In- and Outpatient Care Programs

Sexaholics Anonymous: sa.org

Sex and Love Addicts Anonymous: slaafws.org

Counselors

St. Raphael Counseling: straphaelcounseling.com

Catholic Therapists: catholictherapists.com

Same-Sex Attraction

Courage International: couragerc.org

Eden Invitation: edeninvitation.com

Further Reading

Pornography and Masturbation

Freedom, Everett Fritz

Restored, Matt and Cameron Fradd

Delivered, Matt Fradd

The Porn Myth, Matt Fradd

Dating and Relationships
How to Find Your Soulmate Without Losing Your Soul,
Jason and Crystalina Evert
Emotional Virtue, Sarah Swafford
Dating Detox, Kevin and Lisa Cotter
Men, Women, and the Mystery of Love, Dr. Edward Sri
Theology of the Body in One Hour, Jason Evert

Healing
Be Healed, Bob Schuchts
Unbound, Neal Lozano
I Believe in Love, Fr. Jean C. J. D'Elbee
Made New, Crystalina Evert

Natural Family Planning Apps
Ovulation Mentor (Billings Ovulation Method)
Sympto.org (symptothermal method)
iCycleBeads (Standard Days Method)
LilyPro (symptothermal method)
Lady Cycle (symptothermal method)
myNFP.net (symptothermal method)

About the Authors

 Kelsey Skoch is an international speaker and emcee who shares her faith at Catholic events such as NCYC, SEEK, and World Youth Day. She has served for more than eight years with FOCUS on college campuses and in parishes. Kelsey speaks on the topics of evangelization and missionary discipleship but is best known for her ministry helping women in their personal purity. She resides with her husband and children in Denver, Colorado.

 Everett Fritz is a speaker and bestselling author of multiple books and programs. He has spoken across the country on the topics of discipleship, chastity, and youth ministry. Everett is also the founder and executive director of St. Andrew Missionaries, a ministry that assists Church institutions in shifting their ministry approach with young people. Everett resides in Denver, Colorado, with his wife, Katrina, and their children. To learn more about his ministry, visit standrewmissionaries.org.

ENDNOTES

1   The Barna Group, 2014 Pornography Survey and Statistics.
2   D. Herbenick, J. Bowling, T.C. (Jane) Fu, B. Dodge, L, Guerra-Reyes, S. Sanders, "Sexual Diversity in the United States: Results from a Nationally Representative Probability Sample of Adult Women and Men," PlosOne (2017).
3   L.B. Finer, "Trends in Premarital Sex in the United States," 1954–2003, *Public Health Reports* 122, no. 1 (January–February 2007), 73–78.
4   The Barna Group, 2014 Pornography Survey and Statistics.
5   Herbenick et al., "Sexual Diversity in the United States."
6   Bishop Fulton J. Sheen, *Life Is Worth Living*, revised ed. (San Francisco: Ignatius Press, 1999).
7   John Paul II, *The Theology of the Body: Human Love in the Divine Plan*, reprint ed. (New York: Pauline Books & Media, 1997).
8   Ibid.
9   Rose M. Kreider, and Renee Ellis, "Number, Timing, and Duration of Marriages and Divorces: 2009." Current Population Reports, P70-125 (Washington, DC: U.S. Census Bureau, 2011).
10 Elizabeth Flock, "Devout Catholics Have Better Sex, Study Says," *US News & World Report*, July 17, 2013.
11 Karol Wojtyla, *Love and Responsibility* (San Francisco: Ignatius Press, 1981), 171.
12 "Offenses Against Chastity," in *The Catechism of the Catholic Church*, 2nd ed. (Vatican City: Libreria Editrice Vaticana, 2012).
13 Ibid.
14 Herbenick et al., "Sexual Diversity in the United States."
15 E. Janssen and J. Bancroft, "The Dual-Control Model: The Role of Sexual Inhibition & Excitation in Sexual Arousal and Behavior," in *The Psychophysiology of Sex*, edited by E. Janssen (Bloomington: Indiana University Press, 2007).
16 Simone Kühn and Jürgen Gallinat, "Brain Structure and Functional Connectivity Associated with Pornography Consumption," JAMA Psychiatry 71 (2014):827–34; Valerie Voon et al., "Neural Correlates of Sexual Cue Reactivity in Individuals with and without Compulsive Sexual Behaviours," PlosOne (2014); Dolf Zillmann and Jennings Bryant, "Effects of Massive Exposure to Pornography," in Pornography and Sexual Aggression (New York: Academic Press, 1984); Dolf Zillmann and Jennings Bryant, "Pornography's Impact on Sexual Satisfaction," Journal of Applied Social Psychology 18 (1988): 438–53; Dolf Zillmann and Jennings Bryant, "Effects of Prolonged Consumption of Pornography on Family Values," Journal of Family Issues 9 (1988): 518–44.
17 The Poor Clares of Perpetual Adoration, *Manual for Eucharistic Adoration* (Charlotte, NC: TAN Books, 2016), 129.
18 Mother Teresa, *Where There Is Love, There Is God* (New York: Doubleday, 2010), 191.
19 S.G. Smith, X. Zhang, K.C. Basile, M.T. Merrick, J. Wang, M. Kresnow, J. Chen, The National Intimate Partner and Sexual Violence Survey (NISVS): 2015 Data Brief— Updated Release (Atlanta, GA: National Center for Injury Prevention and Control, Centers for Disease Control and Prevention, 2018).
20 G.K. Chesterton, *What's Wrong with the World* (Mineola, NY: Dover Publications, 2007).

GOT QUESTIONS? GET ANSWERS.

WATCH VIDEOS
GET RELATIONSHIP ADVICE
LAUNCH A PROJECT
READ ANSWERS TO TOUGH QUESTIONS
FIND HELP TO HEAL FROM THE PAST
LISTEN TO POWERFUL TESTIMONIES
SHOP FOR GREAT RESOURCES
SCHEDULE A SPEAKER

Share *UNCOMPROMISING PURITY* with others for as little as

$3 per copy!

Think of those in your community who could benefit from reading it:

- Start a book study in your college dorm
- Give it away in your youth or young adult group
- Share copies with your Confirmation or religious ed classmates
- Study it in your high school religion class
- Distribute copies on retreats
- Offer it as a gift for graduations and birthdays
- Donate copies to your campus ministry program

For more information, visit
chastity.com